THIS book can teach you basic German in the simplest and fastest way. You will learn it here as you would in Germany, by picking it up gradually from everyday incidents and by thinking of them in German. This volume in the LOOK AND LEARN SERIES shows you essential German by the most direct and dramatic means—pictures. The pictures present the incidents in such a way as to lead into direct understanding of the accompanying German expressions. This method is natural to the tourist, it is perfectly suited to the reader taking up German at home, and it is becoming more and more important in the classroom.

EVERY volume in the new LOOK AND LEARN SERIES is written by a prominent teacher especially for this edition. Herbert Lederer, Associate Professor of German at Queens College, has also taught at Ohio University and is the author of numerous articles and book reviews on German literature.

D0889465

*Laurel Look and Learn Series*

LOOK AND LEARN SPANISH
by Francisco Ibarra,
*Director and Professor at the
Academy of Languages,
New York City.*

LOOK AND LEARN FRENCH
by Anna Balakian,
*Professor of French,
New York University.*

LOOK AND LEARN RUSSIAN
by Aron Pressman,
*in Charge of The Department
of Russian, Washington
Square College of Arts and
Sciences, New York University.*

LOOK AND LEARN ITALIAN
by Otis Fellows,
*Professor and Chairman of the
Department of Italian, Columbia University*
and by G. Norman Laidlaw
*Professor and Chairman of Foreign Languages,
Macalester College, St. Paul, Minnesota.*

LOOK AND LEARN ENGLISH
for the Spanish Speaker
by Elena Zayas.

# Look And Learn GERMAN

## HERBERT LEDERER

*Associate Professor of German at Queens College*

*Illustrated by Jack Woolhiser, Jr.*

A LAUREL EDITION

Published by DELL PUBLISHING CO., INC.
1 Dag Hammarskjold Plaza, New York, New York 10017

First printing—November, 1964
Second printing—June, 1970
Third printing—June, 1971
Fourth printing—June, 1973
Fifth printing—January, 1975

Printed in U.S.A.

# Contents

# Author's Note

This book does not claim to teach you to speak German like a native in three easy lessons; no book can do that. Nor will it give you a complete scholarly analysis of the German language. What *Look and Learn German* can and will do, though, is to introduce you to the German language as it is being spoken today.

Since the major emphasis will be on speaking, it is extremely important that you study the pronunciation guide very carefully; practice the pronunciation of all German sounds repeatedly, frequently, and loudly. In this way you will train your ear to recognize and your tongue to pronounce German words.

This method of reading out loud is also essential in the pictorial section. The drawings will give you a good idea of each situation. In most instances, you will be able to understand the caption from the illustrations without having to look up the words in the vocabulary. In any case, do not translate the text into English, but say it in German often enough, so that the German word or phrase will be identified in your mind directly with the thing or the idea for which it stands. Write it down—first copying the text, then from memory. And always say it out loud. This is by far the best way to learn a language: speaking, hearing, reading, and writing.

Don't hurry through the book. Take your time, go through each section slowly and repeatedly until you thoroughly understand and remember all the words, phrases, and idioms. Make up variations of your own. If the text, for instance, says "He is an American," change it to: "I am an American." "She is an American." "We are Americans." "They are not Americans." "Are you an American?" "No, I am not an American." "My wife is an American," and so forth. That way you will acquire active control over the material you have learned, and really make it your own.

At the end of each major section of text, there are questions. Read them out loud, then answer them in German—both in speaking and in writing. (Thinking is not enough.) Then compare your answers with the ones given in the book. Remember that your answer does not have to be identical, for in many instances the answer in the book is not the only answer, but only one possible way of answering the question.

After you have really mastered one section of the text, go on to the next. But always go back to the previous parts, too, and review what you have learned before. You will find that there is a more or less continuous story in the book, dealing with the daily life of an average German family. As you accompany them through a typical day, go to a restaurant or on a trip with them, see them at home and in the office, out shopping or sick in bed, you will learn most of the vocabulary you may need as a tourist, for the reading of simple German texts, or in conversation or correspondence.

You will encounter many forms and endings in the text for which you may not immediately understand the reason. These, of course, are problems of grammar. The grammar section will explain the most important rules and principles of German to you. There are two basic ways of using this section: some people prefer to read the grammar first, so that they have an idea of what they will encounter in the text. Others prefer to read and learn the text first, and memorize forms without knowing the purpose behind them; only afterwards do they turn to the grammatical explanation. I can not tell you which method will work best for you—try it out yourself. Perhaps you will want to combine the two and refer to the grammar section whenever a problem puzzles you.

In any case, while grammatical accuracy is desirable, to be sure, the major purpose of language learning is to understand and to make yourself understood. Don't be afraid of making mistakes. If you don't want to speak until you can speak perfectly, you will have to wait a long time before saying your first word. So go ahead and talk—even at the risk that the Germans may recognize you as an American. And remember that the key to the learning of a language is constant and frequent repetition. A language is a set of habits; and the only way to acquire habits is through practice. Repetition and variation, variation and repetition—that is the only way to do it. And before you know it, you will be able to say: "Look—I have learned German!"

# Look And Learn GERMAN

# Pronunciation Guide

## The German Alphabet

The table below shows the letters of the German alphabet, together with their usual German names; alternate names are given in parentheses.

| | | | | | |
|---|---|---|---|---|---|
| a | *a* | j | *jot* (je) | s | *es* |
| ä | *ä* (Umlaut a) | k | *ka* | ss | *es-zet* (scharfes s) |
| b | *be* | l | *el* | t | *te* |
| c | *ce* | m | *em* | u | *u* |
| d | *de* | n | *en* | ü | *ü* (Umlaut u) |
| e | *e* | o | *o* | v | *vau* |
| f | *ef* | ö | *ö* (Umlaut o) | w | *we* |
| g | *ge* | p | *pe* | x | *ix* |
| h | *ha* | q | *ku* (que) | y | *ypsilon* |
| i | *i* | r | *er* | z | *zet* |

As you can see from this table, German has four letters which do not exist in English: the vowels ä, ö, and ü, which we will discuss later, and the consonant ß. The latter, in handwriting and typing, is frequently replaced by a double s, as it has been in this book.

## The German Sounds

German is a more nearly phonetic language than English. Basically, each letter represents a single sound, and each sound is symbolized by a single letter; there are very few exceptions to this principle. In contrast, in English the letters "ough" represent very different sounds in the words though, through, cough, tough, bough, and hiccoughs. Conversely, the sound "ee" can be represented by different letters or letter combinations in such words as three, sea, me, receive, believe, machine.

## Vowels

For all practical purposes, the pronunciation of German vowels and vowel combinations varies only in length, but not in quality. In other words, a German vowel may be long or short, but the basic sound is the same. Thus, the German *a* is always pronounced "ah" as in the English word *father,* never as in the English words *gate* or *man* or *law*. Also, German vowels do not contain the sliding or slurring quality of many English vowels; the German word *so,* for example, never ends up with the sound "oo", as does the English word *so*.

In general, German vowels are long if there are two of them together, if they are followed by an *h* (which is silent after a vowel), or by a single consonant. A vowel is short when followed by more than one consonant or when it occurs in an unstressed final syllable, with or without a following consonant. In the table below, the first line contains several examples for the long pronunciation, the second line for the short pronunciation of each vowel. The suggested English pronunciation equivalents are, of course, only approximations, but they will give you a sufficient idea of the way each vowel sounds.

SIMPLE VOWELS:

| German symbol | Approximate English equivalent | Examples |
|---|---|---|
| a | "ah" | Vater, Paar, fahren |
| | | alt, Mann, Sofa |
| e | "eh" | geben, leer, zehn |
| | | Geld, Bett, Rose |

| German symbol | Approximate English equivalent | Examples |
|---|---|---|
| i | "ee" | mir, ihn |
| | | bitte, finden, wenig |
| o | "oh" | oben, Boot, Sohn |
| | | Post, Sonne, Radio |
| u | "oo" | Schule, Schuh |
| | | Mund, Mutter, Übung |

*Vowel combinations (always long):*

| | | |
|---|---|---|
| au | "ow" | Haus, Auge, Frau |
| ei | "eye" | mein, zwei |
| ie | "ee" | die, sieht |
| eu, äu | "oy" | heute, Häuser |

VOWEL VARIATIONS:

There are three German vowel variations, indicated by two dots or short lines over the letters a, o, and u: ä, ö, ü. These are called *Umlaut.* The long *ä* is roughly equivalent to the sound of the English word *bear;* the short *ä* is identical with the sound of the German *e.*

The *ö* and *ü* sounds have no English equivalent. The *ö* sounds like the French "eu". It is produced by rounding the lips as for the German *o,* but putting the tongue in the position to say the German *e.*

Similarly, the *ü* sound, which corresponds to the French "u", is produced by rounding the lips as if to pronounce the German *u,* while having the tongue in the position for pronouncing the German *i.* With a little practice, preferably in front of a mirror, you will be able to master these sounds.

Again, we list examples for a long pronunciation in the first line, a short pronunciation in the second line:

| | |
|---|---|
| ä | Bär, nähren |
| | Männer, älter |
| ö | Öl, Söhne |
| | Hölle, öfter |
| ü | Tür, führen |
| | füllen, fünf |

The German letter y is never a consonant, but always a vowel, pronounced like the German ü: *lyrisch*.

VOWEL SEPARATION:
A word that begins with a vowel must be clearly separated from the last consonant of the preceding word by a short pause. Contrast the English phrases "an ice man" and "a nice man" to get this feeling of separation.


## Consonants

| German symbol | Explanation | Examples |
|---|---|---|
| b | at the beginning or in the middle of a word, as in English; at the end of a word or syllable and before t, like English *p*. | Bär, aber<br><br>ob, abnehmen, gibt |
| c | occurs by itself only in words of foreign origin, where the original pronunciation is preserved. | Café, Cello, Crème |
| ch | no exact English equivalent; similar to an *h* pronounced with a lot of friction in the throat, as in *humor;*<br>in a few words of foreign origin, original pronunciation is preserved. | ich, ach, Buch<br><br>Chaos, Chauffeur |
| chs | ks | Fuchs |
| ck | as in English. | dick |

| German symbol | *Explanation* | *Examples* |
|---|---|---|
| d | at the beginning or in the middle of a word, as in English; | dick, dann, oder |
| | at the end of a word or syllable and before t, like English *t*. | Hand, Mädchen, Stadt |
| f | as in English. | fallen |
| g | at the beginning or in the middle of a word, as in English *go* (never as in *general*); | gehen, fragen, gibt |
| | in a few words of French origin, as in French *rouge;* | rouge, Genie |
| | at the end of a word or syllable and before t, like English *k;* | Tag, weggehen, legt |
| | but in the final syllable *-ig,* like German *-ich.* | wenig |
| gn | both pronounced. | Gnade |
| h | at the beginning of a word or syllable, as in English; | Herr, gehören |
| | after a vowel, silent. | zehn, sehen |
| j | like English *y* in *yes.* | ja, Jahr |
| k | as in English. | kein, klein |
| kn | both pronounced. | Knie |
| l | basically as in English, although the tongue is closer to the teeth. | lang, alles |
| m | as in English. | Mutter, am |

| German symbol | Explanation | Examples |
|---|---|---|
| n | as in English. | nein, in |
| ng | as in English *singer,* never as in English *finger.* | singen, Finger |
| p | as in English. | Paul, Kappe |
| pf | both pronounced. | Pferd, Apfel |
| q | like English *k-v.* | Quelle |
| r | more of a trilled or rolled sound than in English, especially *rr;* | rot, Arbeit, Herr |
| | but in unstressed final syllable, similar to English. | Bruder, aber |
| s | at the end of a word or syllable or before a consonant, as in English; | Gas, Wasser, beste |
| | before a vowel, like English *z.* | Rose, sehr |
| sch | like English *sh.* | Schuh, Schule, Busch |
| sh | does not exist. If it occurs accidentally at the juncture of two words, *s* and *h* are pronounced separately. | Glashaus |
| sp | at the beginning of a word, like English *sh-p;* | spielen |
| | otherwise as in English. | Wespe |
| st | at the beginning of a word, like English *sh-t;* | Stein, Stadt |
| | otherwise as in English. | Nest |

| German symbol | Approximate English equivalent | Examples |
|---|---|---|
| ß(ss) | like English *ss*. | daß, Füße |
| t | as in English. | Tür, rot |
| th | like English *t*. | Theater, Goethe |
| -tion | like English *tsee-on*. | Nation |
| tt | like English *t*, never soft. | Butter, bitte |
| tz | like English *t-s*. | Netz, jetzt |
| v | like English *f*; in a few words of foreign origin, as in English. | Vater, viel November |
| w | like English *v*. | wann, schwer |
| z | like English *t-s*. | zehn, zwei |

## Stress

Most German words are stressed on the first syllable of the stem; prefixes carry stress only if they have independent meaning of their own. In the following words, the stressed syllable is followed by an accent mark: *ste'hen; verste'hen; auf'stehen.* The second and the third are compounds of the verb *stehen* (to stand). The prefix *ver-* has no meaning of its own and thus does not carry stress; on the other hand, the prefix *auf-* does have meaning (it means "up," and *aufstehen* is "to stand up"), and therefore it receives the stress.

Words of foreign origin are usually stressed on the last syllable. Again, we show this by an accent mark: *Universi-*

*tät'*, *Student'*, *Paris'*, *Automat'*, *Republik'*, etc. There are, however, a few exceptions from this rule, where the original stress of a foreign word is maintained: *Profes'sor, Exa'men*.

Remember that this accent does not occur in the language; it is used only as a teaching aid here. There are no accent marks in German, except in foreign words like *Café*.

## Syllabication

A word has as many syllables as it has vowels or vowel combinations. Usually a syllable begins with a single consonant. However, consonant clusters like *ch* or *sch* are not separated. There are no silent syllables in German; all final vowels are pronounced.

## Capitalization

German not only capitalizes the first word of each sentence and all proper names, as does English, but also all common nouns and all forms of the pronoun *Sie* (you). On the other hand, *ich* (I) is not capitalized, nor are adjectives denoting nationality.

## Punctuation

By and large, German punctuation marks are used as in English. The comma, however, must be used to set off all dependent clauses, including relative clauses and infinitive phrases:

> Ich weiss nicht, ob er kommt.
> Das Buch, das ich lese, ist interessant.
> Es ist schwer, gut Deutsch zu sprechen.

On the other hand, single words like however, nevertheless, etc., or phrases like two weeks ago, in my opinion, on the other hand, are *not* set off by commas in German.

Commas are used as in English to separate words in a series, but are omitted before the word *und* (and):

The colors of the American flag are red,
white, and blue.

Die Farben der amerikanischen Fahne sind rot,
weiß und blau.

# Grammar

The grammar of a language is the system by means of which individual words are joined into meaningful utterances. A "law" or rule of grammar is not like a natural law, such as the law of gravity, which can not be broken, nor is it like a man-made law, such as traffic regulations, which should not be broken for fear of paying the consequences. Linguistic laws are merely observations as to how a given language behaves under given circumstances. The rules of grammar are statements of principles on which the structure of the language is based. The more of these principles you understand and are able to apply, the better you will learn the language.

German grammar differs from English grammar in two fundamental respects: German is a more highly inflected language, *i.e.* the nouns, verbs, and adjectives have a greater variety of endings, and the German word order is more complex, especially the position of the verb. These then are the problems that we must keep most clearly in mind: What is the form of this word, and where does it go in the sentence? Let us first turn our attention to basic forms:

## 1. Articles and Pronouns

To begin with, German has three genders: masculine, feminine, and neuter. In English, these exist only as pronouns (he, she, and it); in German, every noun has a gender, and the distribution is arbitrary. Natural sex has practically nothing to do with it. While it is true that almost all nouns denoting male human beings are masculine, it does not follow that all nouns denoting female human beings are feminine;

as a matter of fact, some of the most common words, such as *Fräulein* (Miss) or *Mädchen* (girl) are neuter. On the other hand, all inanimate objects are by no means neuter; many are masculine or feminine. There is no reason that a table should be masculine, a wall feminine, or a window neuter. Nor is it logical that a spoon is masculine, a knife neuter, and a fork feminine. But then you must not expect reason or logic in language—a language is what it is, and there is no point in arguing. The gender of each noun must be memorized with the noun.

The following table will illustrate the various forms of the article:

|  | Masculine | Neuter | Feminine | All Plurals |
|---|---|---|---|---|
| definite article (the) | d*er* | das | die | die |
| indefinite article (a, an) | ein | ein | ein*e* | ———— |
| not a, not any | kein | kein | kein*e* | kein*e* |

*Kein* is the negative form of the indefinite article:
Ich habe ein Buch
— I have a book
Ich habe kein Buch
— I have no book, I haven't any book
Das ist ein Fenster
— That is a window
Das ist kein Fenster
— That is not a window, that is no window

You may have noticed that the masculine and neuter forms are sometimes identical and that feminine and plural are often the same. The latter is also the case with pronouns (he, she, it, they). In fact, as you see from the endings in italics, article and pronoun forms correspond:

| Masculine | Neuter | Feminine | All Plurals |
|---|---|---|---|
| *er* | *es* | si*e* | si*e* |

Please note that *sie* can mean either "she" or "they." Usually the verb ending will help you distinguish between the two; otherwise you have to rely on context.

Each noun must be replaced by a pronoun of the same gender. Thus, *der Mann* (the man) is referred to by the pronoun *er* (he). The same pronoun *er,* however, also refers to *der Tisch* (the table), and then corresponds to English "it." Similarly, *sie* means "she" when the word refers to a woman (*die Frau—sie*), but *sie* means "it" when the word, for instance, refers to a fork (*die Gabel—sie*) or any other feminine noun. When the word *sie* replaces a plural noun, it corresponds to the English word "they."

To understand the meaning of a pronoun, you must therefore know the noun to which it refers. It will always have the same gender.

The personal pronouns *ich* (I), *wir* (we), and *Sie* (you, singular and plural) have no gender and do not vary. On the other hand, possessive, demonstrative, and similar adjectives do have gender and show the distinctive endings of the pronouns:

|  | *Masculine* | *Neuter* | *Feminine* | *All Plurals* |
|---|---|---|---|---|
| this | dies*er* | dies*es* | dies*e* | dies*e* |
| that | jen*er* | jen*es* | jen*e* | jen*e* |
| which | welch*er* | welch*es* | welch*e* | welch*e* |
| every | jed*er* | jed*es* | jed*e* | jed*e* |

The possessives, like *ein* and *kein,* have no endings for masculine and neuter:

| my | mein | mein | mein*e* | mein*e* |
|---|---|---|---|---|
| our | unser | unser | unser*e* | unser*e* |
| his, its | sein | sein | sein*e* | sein*e* |
| her, their (its) | ihr | ihr | ihr*e* | ihr*e* |
| your | Ihr | Ihr | Ihr*e* | Ihr*e* |

Just as is the case with the article, the possessive must agree with the noun to which it refers. Therefore, *sein* and *ihr* can mean "its" when they refer to inanimate objects. Thus, *"der* Mann und *sein* Sohn" means "the man and his son," but *"das* Zimmer und *sein* Fenster" means "the room and its window." Similarly, *"die* Frau und *ihre* Tochter" means "the woman and her daughter," while *"die* Lampe und *ihre* Farbe" means "the lamp and its color." While the choice of the correct word (*sein, ihr*) depends on the noun to which it refers, the choice of ending depends on the noun which follows.

Notice that all forms of "you" and "your" (*Sie, Ihr,* etc.) are always capitalized in German.

## 2. *Noun Plurals*

We have learned that every noun has a gender in the singular, and must be learned together with its article: *der Tisch* (the table), *das Buch* (the book), *die Tür* (the door). We have also seen that the definite article and all words derived from it have only one form for the plural of all genders: *die.* There are, however, several ways to show noun plurals. We will discuss the four most common ones here.

A) Some nouns do not add any ending in the plural, but may have a change in the stem vowel, a so-called *Umlaut:* a becomes *ä, o* becomes *ö, u* becomes *ü.* (Compare English sheep—sheep, no change, or foot—feet, vowel change.)

*Examples:*

| | | |
|---|---|---|
| der Lehrer | die Lehrer | (teacher) |
| das Mädchen | die Mädchen | (girl) |
| das Fenster | die Fenster | (window) |
| der Vogel | die Vögel | (bird) |
| der Laden | die Läden | (store) |
| die Mutter | die Mütter | (mother) |

This group consists mainly of masculine and neuter nouns that end in *-el, -en,* and *-er,* neuter nouns that end in *-chen* and *-lein,* and two feminine nouns: *Mutter* and *Tochter* (daughter). The two feminine nouns in this group also take an *Umlaut* in the plural, the neuter nouns never do, and the masculines sometimes.

B) Some nouns add the ending *-e,* occasionally with an *Umlaut* in the stem.

*Examples:*

| | | |
|---|---|---|
| der Tag | die Tage | (day) |
| der Fuss | die Füsse | (foot) |
| die Stadt | die Städte | (city) |
| das Jahr | die Jahre | (year) |
| der Monat | die Monate | (month) |

This group contains mainly one-syllable masculine and feminine nouns, a few one-syllable neuter nouns, and some very few multisyllabic nouns. Again, the neuter nouns never take an *Umlaut,* the feminine do whenever possible, and with the masculine ones you can't be sure.

C) Some nouns add the ending *-er,* with *Umlaut* in the stem whenever possible.

*Examples:*

| | | |
|---|---|---|
| das Kind | die Kinder | (child) |
| das Buch | die Bücher | (book) |
| der Mann | die Männer | (man) |

This group contains mainly one-syllable neuter nouns and a few one-syllable masculine nouns, but no feminines.

D) Some nouns add the ending *-en* (or *-n* only, if the *-e* is already there). These nouns never change the stem vowel.

*Examples:*

| | | |
|---|---|---|
| der Junge | die Jungen | (boy) |
| der Student | die Studenten | (student) |
| die Schule | die Schulen | (school) |
| die Tür | die Türen | (door) |

In this group we find mostly masculine and feminine

nouns of two or more syllables, and a few one-syllable masculines and feminines, but no neuters.

Some very few nouns are irregular. An *-s* as a sign of the plural, however, which we are accustomed to in English, is exceedingly rare and found only on a few technical words, such as *das Radio—die Radios* or *das Auto—die Autos*. On the whole, it is best to learn the plural of each noun.

## 3. The Verb

The verb is the key to the German sentence. We will concern ourselves first with the simplest and most common form, the present tense, which is used throughout the text of this book.

### A) The Present Tense

The two most important German verbs are the verbs *sein* (to be) and *haben* (to have). Here are their present tense forms:

|                      |                     |
| -------------------- | ------------------- |
| *sein*               |                     |
| ich bin              | I am                |
| er (sie, es) ist     | he (she, it) is     |
| wir, sie, Sie sind   | we, they, you are   |
|                      |                     |
| *haben*              |                     |
| ich habe             | I have              |
| er (sie, es) hat     | he (she, it) has    |
| wir, sie, Sie haben  | we, they, you have  |

As you can see from these examples, there are three basic forms for each verb: first person singular: *ich* (I), third person singular: *er, sie, es* (he, she, it), and the general form which serves for the first and third person plural: *wir, sie* (we, they), and for the second person, both singular and plural: *Sie* (you). This is the so-called polite form of the second person and the one you will be most likely to see, hear, and use. There are two other forms, which are less frequent and which we will discuss later.

Let us see how the above forms apply to other verbs. The infinitive (the way a verb is listed in the vocabulary) also serves as the general form (we, they, and you) in the present tense:

singen — to sing                    wir singen — we sing
Sie singen — you sing            sie singen — they sing

As with the verb *haben,* the first person singular usually ends in *-e,* the third person in *-t.*

ich singe — I sing
er, sie, es singt — he, she, it sings

This is true of almost all verbs in the present tense. Take for instance the verb *kommen* (to come):

ich komme — I come
er, sie, es kommt — he, she, it comes
wir, sie, Sie kommen — we, they, you come

There are a few minor variations. If, for instance, the stem of a verb ends in *-d* or *-t,* the ending in the third person singular becomes *-et,* to make it audible:

antworten — to answer          er antwortet — he answers
finden — to find                        sie findet — she finds

A few verbs undergo a vowel change in the third person singular, similar to the English verb "I do"—he does. Thus, an *a* in the infinitive may become an *ä* in the 3rd person, and an *e* may turn into an *i* or an *ie.* There are no hard and fast rules about which verbs have such changes. When they do, the changes are indicated in the vocabulary. Here are a few examples:

fahren — to drive          ich fahre          er fährt
geben — to give            ich gebe           er gibt
sehen — to see             ich sehe           er sieht

In addition, some very few verbs have irregular endings or no endings in the singular. (All German verbs are regular in the plural, which, except for the verb *sein* (to be) is identical with the infinitive.) Remember the following irregular verbs:

| | | |
|---|---|---|
| werden — to become | ich werde | er wird |
| wissen — to know | ich weiss | er weiss |
| müssen — to have to | ich muss | er muss |
| können — to be able | ich kann | er kann |
| wollen — to want to | ich will | er will |
| sollen — to be supposed to | ich soll | er soll |
| dürfen — to be allowed to | ich darf | er darf |
| mögen — to like, may | ich mag | er mag |

The last six of these verbs are called "modals." We will come back to them later.

Since all German verbs have different forms in the singular and in the plural, and since the verb must always agree with the subject, it will be easy to find out when *sie* means she and when it means they:

| | |
|---|---|
| sie hat — she has | sie haben — they have |
| sie kommt — she comes | sie kommen — they come |
| sie bringt — she brings | sie bringen — they bring |
| sie kann — she can | sie können — they can |
| sie sieht — she sees | sie sehen — they see |

On the other hand, *Sie* meaning "you" is always capitalized: *Sie haben* — you have; *Sie kommen* — you come; *Sie bringen* — you bring; *Sie können* — you can; *Sie sehen* — you see.

German has only *one* present tense form. Thus *ich lese* may be expressed in English as "I read," "I am reading," or "I do read." *Er singt* means "he sings," "he is singing," or "he does sing."

Commands are formed in German in a very simple fashion: We add *Sie* (you) to the infinitive or general form.

| | |
|---|---|
| Kommen Sie! | Come! |
| Bringen Sie! | Bring! |

| | |
|---|---|
| Zeigen Sie! | Show! |
| Lesen Sie! | Read! |
| Antworten Sie mir! | Answer me! |
| Sprechen Sie langsam! | Speak slowly! |

Normally, of course, we would add *bitte* (please) either before or after the command.

A German verb is negated simply by adding the word *nicht* (not): *Ich habe nicht* — I have not; *sie kann nicht* — she can not; *ich gehe nicht* — I do not go; *er kommt nicht* — he is not coming; *wir arbeiten nicht* — we are not working, we do not work; *Spielen Sie nicht!* — Don't play!

Similarly, in order to ask a question, we simply reverse the position of subject and verb:

| | |
|---|---|
| Sie können — you can | Können Sie? — Can you? |
| Er geht — He goes | Geht er? — Does he go? |
| Sie singt — She is singing | Singt sie? — Is she singing? |

Wann kommt der nächste Zug?
 — When does the next train come?
Was tue ich? — What am I doing?
Wo arbeiten Sie? — Where do you work?

This brings us to an extremely important point: the position of the verb. In English, the verb usually follows the subject. In German, this is not necessarily the case. A German sentence may, to be sure, begin with the subject and follow it with the verb:

Der Mann ist hier — The man is here
Er kam gestern — He came yesterday
Es ist jetzt 10 Uhr — It is now ten o'clock

If, however, the German sentence begins with anything *other* than the subject (except for the conjunctions *and*, *but*, and *or*), the subject follows the verb:

Hier ist der Mann — Here is the man
Gestern kam er — Yesterday he came
Jetzt ist es 10 Uhr — Now it is ten o'clock

This is also the case, as we have seen, for commands and questions, which either begin with the verb itself or with an interrogatory. Here again, the subject follows the verb:

Kommen Sie her! — Come here!
Bringen Sie mir ein Glas Bier!
    — Bring me a glass of beer!
Arbeiten Sie heute? — Are you working today?
Singt sie nicht schön? — Doesn't she sing beautifully?
Wann geht der nächste Zug?
    — When does the next train leave?

To put it differently: only one element may come before the verb. (An element may be a word, a phrase, or a clause.) If this element is not the subject, then the subject must come after the verb. We can illustrate this as follows:

*Normal word order:* S — V — O (Subject, Verb, Object)
*Inverted word order:* x — V — S — O, where x is
    anything other than the subject.

Just to make it more complicated, however, not *all* of the verb will be in this position. If a German predicate (the entire verb complex) consists of two or more parts, the first of these will be in its normal position, the others will come at the end of the sentence or clause. You must get used to this "split-verb" phenomenon; in fact, it is a very good idea to train yourself always to check the end of the sentence for additional information about the verb.

In English, for instance, I can either say "He takes his hat off" or "He takes off his hat." In German, I must say: "Er *nimmt* seinen Hut *ab*." Another example: the German word for "to get up" is *aufstehen*. "I get up" is "Ich stehe *auf*."

      I get up at six o'clock
          — Ich stehe um 6 Uhr *auf*.
      I always get up at 6 o'clock
          — Ich stehe immer um 6 Uhr *auf*.

These are called "separable prefixes." Notice that the infinitive (and this is the form you have to look up in a vocabulary or dictionary) begins with the prefix; *aufstehen* (to get up) has to be looked up under the letter *a*. But when it is used in a sentence, as the above examples show, the prefix comes at the end. In the vocabulary of this book, separable prefixes will be indicated by a dot between the prefix and the stem, *i.e., auf·stehen*. Remember that this is merely a device for your convenience—the Germans don't write it that way.

The separable prefixes can be recognized by the fact that the prefix is an adverb or a preposition that can have independent meaning. The following prefixes, which do not have independent meaning, can never be separated from the verb stem: *be-, emp-, ent-, er-, ge-, miss-, ver-, zer-*.

Later on, when we come to the perfect tense (I have seen) and the future tense (he will go), we will see that since they always consist of two verbs, the second part of the predicate will always be found at the end of the sentence or clause. The same is also true when one of the modals (*können, müssen, wollen, sollen, dürfen, mögen*) is used with another verb: the second verb is in the infinitive and comes at the end of the sentence or clause.

> I want to read — Ich will lesen
> I want to read the book — Ich will das Buch
> lesen
> I want to read the book now
> — Ich will das Buch jetzt lesen
> I don't want to read the book now
> — Ich will das Buch jetzt nicht lesen

## B) *The Past Tense*

Up to now, we have discussed the present tense of verbs; there are, however, other tenses. Basically, they are not difficult, and after you have learned them, you can change the caption of any picture in the text to the past or the future, and practice these forms as well.

Let us begin with the past. In English, some verbs form

their past tense in a regular fashion, by adding an ending
(work—worked, live—lived, play—played, etc.), while
others are irregular by changing their stem in some way
(come—came, sing—sang, is—was, go—went, bring—
brought). German verbs behave in the same way. In fact,
the verbs that are regular in English are usually also regular
in German, and vice versa. The regular verbs add the ending
-*te* in the singular, -*ten* in the plural:

| | | |
|---|---|---|
| *spielen* (to play) | ich, er, sie, es spiel*te*; wir, sie, Sie spiel*ten* | I (etc.) played<br>we (etc.) played |
| *leben* (to live) | ich, er, sie, es leb*te*; wir, sie, Sie leb*ten* | I (etc.) lived<br>we (etc.) lived |

The basic model for the endings of these verbs is the helping
verb *haben* (to have):

| | |
|---|---|
| ich, er, sie, es hat*te* | I, he, she, it had |
| wir, sie, Sie hat*ten* | we, they, you had |

If the stem of a verb already ends in a -*d* or -*t*, we insert
an -*e*- before the ending to make it pronounceable:

   *arbeiten* (to work)   sing.: arbeit*ete*   plural: arbeit*eten*

Irregular verbs usually change their stem vowel to show
past tense (drive—drove, find—found), but have no ending. The same is true in German; these verbs change their
stem vowel, have no ending in the singular, and an -*en*
ending in the plural.

| | | |
|---|---|---|
| *kommen* (to come) | ich, er, sie, es kam; wir, sie, Sie kam*en* | I, he, she, it came<br>we, they, you came |
| *singen* (to sing) | ich, er, sie, es sang; wir, sie, Sie sang*en* | I (etc.) sang<br>we (etc.) sang |

| *fahren* (to drive) | ich, er, sie, es fuhr; wir, sie, Sie fuhr*en* | I (etc.) drove we (etc.) drove |
|---|---|---|

Some few verbs show an even greater irregularity: they do not merely change the vowel, but the entire stem (as, for instance, the English verb to go—went). Here are the most important ones in German. We list only the infinitive and the singular past tense; the plural merely adds *-en* or *-n:*

| | |
|---|---|
| sein (to be) | war (was) |
| gehen (to go) | ging (went) |
| tun (to do) | tat (did) |
| werden (to become) | wurde (became) |
| sitzen (to sit) | sass (sat) |
| bringen (to bring) | brachte (brought) |
| denken (to think) | dachte (thought) |
| stehen (to stand) | stand (stood) |

The modals, which we will discuss later, also have slight irregularities in the past tense. The table of irregular verbs in back of the book will show you the forms of the most important German verbs.

## C) The Perfect Tense

The present and the past are called "simple tenses," because there is only one verb form involved. Now we come to the so-called compound tenses, which use a helping verb. First, let us discuss the perfect (I have played, she has sung). Again exactly as in English, the German verb will have two parts: the helping verb *haben* (to have), and the past participle of the main verb (played, sung, etc.). The past participle will either be regular or irregular. In German, almost all past participles begin with the prefix *ge-*. The regular verbs add the ending *-t* to the stem, without changing the vowel.

Here are a few examples showing the three basic forms (called "principal parts") of some regular verbs: the infinitive, the third person singular past, and the past participle with the helping verb.

| spielen (to play) | spielte | hat *ge*spiel*t* |
| leben (to live) | lebte | hat *ge*leb*t* |
| antworten (to answer) | antwortete | hat *ge*antwort*et* |

The last example again shows the insertion of the linking -*e*-between stem and ending, if the stem ends in -*t*.

Strong verbs, on the other hand, have the same *ge*- prefix, but change the stem vowel and add an -*en* ending. Here are some examples of principle parts:

| singen (to sing) | sang | hat *ge*sung*en* |
| schreiben (to write) | schrieb | hat *ge*schrieb*en* |
| lesen (to read) | las | hat *ge*les*en* |

So far, the pattern is exactly the same as in English. There are some verbs, however, that do not use the helping verb *haben* (to have), but rather the verb *sein* (to be) with the past participle; this is similar to the English phrase "he *is* gone," but is more widespread. Thus, for example, we say in German:

> er *ist* gekommen — he has come
> ich *bin* gegangen — I have gone

These verbs all have one thing in common: they are intransitive, that is, they have no direct object. They include first of all many common verbs of motion, such as *kommen* (to come) and *gehen* (to go) listed above, or *laufen* (to run), *fliegen* (to fly), *fahren* (to drive or travel), *schwimmen* (to swim) and their compounds. Also included are some verbs showing change of condition, such as *werden* (to become) — *ist geworden* (has become), *wachsen* (to grow), *sterben* (to die), *aufwachen* (to wake up), *einschlafen* (to fall asleep), etc. Finally, there are a few other important verbs that follow this pattern: *sein* (to be) — *sie sind gewesen* (they have been); *bleiben* (to stay) — *wir sind geblieben* (we have stayed); *geschehen* (to happen) — *was ist geschehen?* (what has happened?).

In the table of irregular verbs, all these verbs which form their perfect tense with the helping verb *sein* are identified by the word *ist* before the past participle.

Whatever the helping verb, the past participle will be placed at the end of the sentence or clause:

> Ich habe den Mann gestern gesehen
> — I have seen the man yesterday
> Er ist in mein Zimmer gekommen
> — He has come into my room

When a verb begins with one of the so-called inseparable prefixes (*be-, ent-, emp-, er-, ge-, miss-, ver-, zer-*), or when it ends with the letters *-ieren*, the past participle does *not* add the prefix *ge-*. Here are a few examples:

> bekommen (to get, receive)
> — Ich habe ein Buch bekommen
> verstehen (to understand)
> —Haben Sie die Frage verstanden?
> erzählen (to tell) — Er hat eine Geschichte erzählt
> studieren (to study) — Wir haben Deutsch studiert

On the other hand, verbs with the so-called separable prefixes (all those which have independent meaning) insert the syllable *-ge-* in the past participle between the prefix and the stem. The following examples will show you how this works:

> abnehmen (to take off)
> — Er hat seinen Hut ab*ge*nommen
> aufstehen (to get up)
> — Ich bin um sechs Uhr auf*ge*standen
> anfangen (to start)
> — Der Film hat schon an*ge*fangen

German does not differentiate very clearly between the past tense (*ich spielte* — I played), and the present perfect (*ich habe gespielt* — I have played). For all practical purposes, they are interchangeable, and you can use either one.

In general, the Germans prefer the past tense for formal, written usage, and the perfect tense for informal, conversational speech. But this rule is not absolute. When it comes to speaking German, use whichever form comes easier to you, and you will be understood.

While the vowel changes of irregular verbs can not always be predicted completely, there are nevertheless some major patterns into which most verbs fall. The following table may help you. It shows the most important types of vowel variations, listing for each group the vowel of the infinitive, past tense, and past participle. (The English verb "to sing", for example, would be listed as i—a—u, to show the forms sing—sang—sung.)

| Infinitive | Past Tense | Past Participle | Examples |
|---|---|---|---|
| a | ie *or* u | a | schlafen (to sleep) |
| | | | fahren (to drive) |
| e | a | e *or* o | geben (to give) |
| | | | helfen (to help) |
| ei | ie *or* i | ie *or* i | schreiben (to write) |
| | | | reiten (to ride) |
| i | a | u *or* o | singen (to sing) |
| | | | beginnen (to begin) |
| ie | o | o | fliegen (to fly) |

The vast majority of irregular German verbs will follow one of these patterns. But here are the principal parts of the twelve most important German verbs, which can not be classified into any of these groups:

| | | |
|---|---|---|
| bringen (to bring) | brachte | hat gebracht |
| denken (to think) | dachte | hat gedacht |
| essen (to eat) | ass | hat gegessen |
| gehen (to go) | ging | ist gegangen |
| kommen (to come) | kam | ist gekommen |
| liegen (to lie down) | lag | hat gelegen |
| sein (to be) | war | ist gewesen |
| sitzen (to sit) | sass | hat gesessen |

| stehen (to stand) | stand | hat gestanden |
| tun (to do) | tat | hat getan |
| werden (to become) | wurde | ist geworden |
| wissen (to know) | wusste | hat gewusst |

Again, we refer you to the table of irregular verbs for a more complete listing.

## D) The Future

The other important compound tense is the future. (We will not discuss the past perfect and the future perfect in this book.) The future is formed with a helping verb (English "shall" or "will") and an infinitive: I shall play, he will help, etc. Once again, the basic pattern is the same in German. The helping verb is the present tense of *werden,* which actually means "to become" and thus implies that which is to be, but is not yet, hence the future. The infinitive, as we would expect, comes at the end of the clause or sentence.

A few examples should suffice to illustrate the principle:

> Ich werde morgen Tennis spielen
> — I shall play tennis tomorrow
> Er wird mir helfen
> — He will help me
> Wir werden am Abend ins Kino gehen
> — We will go to the movies tonight
> Werden Sie mit uns kommen?
> — Will you come with us?

As in English, German often uses the present tense to imply a future action, if the time sequence is clear from the context:

> Ich gehe morgen ins Theater
> — I am going to the theater tomorrow
> Mein Zug fährt um 5 Uhr
> — My train leaves at 5 o'clock

## E) Modal Verbs

We now come to those special verbs, the modals, which we

have mentioned before. There are six of them, and they are very important. Since their meanings do not always correspond to similar English verbs, it is best to think of them as expressing a certain function or idea, and then find the English word or phrase that corresponds to this idea.

*Wollen* implies wish or desire. It does *not* express the future; as we have seen, the German verb *werden* does that. Thus we find that *er wird gehen* means "he will go"; *er will gehen,* however, means "he wants to go." Keep this difference clearly in mind.

*Können* implies ability. Therefore *ich kann* means "I can, I am able"; *wir können nicht* means "we can not."

*Müssen* implies obligation. It is best translated as "to have to." Thus, *ich muss gehen* means "I have to go." The negative of *müssen* merely stands for the lack of obligation. *Er muss nicht kommen* therefore means that "he does not have to come." It does not correspond to the idea that "he must not come," which is an entirely different concept.

*Dürfen* implies permission. This is often expressed in English with the word "may": *Darf ich ein Glas Wasser haben?* (May I have a glass of water?). It follows logically that the negative of *dürfen* stands for the absence of permission: *Sie dürfen das nicht tun* means "you are not permitted to do that," and hence corresponds to the English "you must not do that."

*Sollen* implies "to be supposed to." This may refer to some kind of moral obligation, such as *Ich soll um 10 Uhr nach Hause kommen* (I am supposed to come home at 10 o'clock). It may also indicate a certain reputation, as in the sentence *Er soll sehr reich sein* (He is supposed to be very rich).

*Mögen,* finally, has two basic meanings. It either implies liking, as in *Mögen Sie dieses Buch nicht?* (Don't you like this book?) or possibility, as in *Dies mag wahr sein* (This may be true).

Always keep these basic meanings in mind. And notice that in all the examples given above, the modal is used together with some other verb. This other verb is in the infinitive and is found at the end of the sentence or the clause.

Contrary to English, where the modals are limited in their tense forms ("can" exists only in the present and past tenses, "must" only in the present), the German modals have all tenses. Here are their past tense forms; notice that *sollen* and *wollen* are regular, while the others drop the *Umlaut*. *Mögen* also changes the consonants of the stem:

dürfen—durfte      müssen—musste
können—konnte      sollen—sollte
mögen—mochte      wollen—wollte

In the compound tenses, the modals are characterized by a special form that we call the "double infinitive," that is, two infinitives at the end of the sentence or clause, first the regular verb, then the modal. Thus, for example, in the future, modals look like this:

Ich werde mit ihm *gehen können*
    — I shall be able to go with him
Er wird den Brief *schreiben müssen*
    — He will have to write the letter

The same thing is true in the perfect tense, with a form of *haben* and the double infinitive at the end:

Er hat seine Grosseltern *sehen wollen*
    — He has wanted to see his grandparents
Sie hat nicht mit ihrer Freundin *spielen dürfen*
    — She has not been permitted to play with
       her girlfriend

## 4. *The Case System*

In English, only a few pronouns show differences between subject and object by a change in form, such as I—me, we—us, he—him, etc. In fact, in colloquial speech today, this distinction is no longer very sharp. In German, however, such variations exist not only for pronouns, but for nouns, articles, and adjectives as well. These are called "case forms," and they indicate the function of that particular word in the sentence. German has four cases: Nominative, Accusative, Dative, and Genitive. We will discuss them in this order.

## A) Nominative

The nominative is the case of the subject. Its forms, which we have discussed before, are *der, das,* and *die* for the singular of the definite article, *sie* for the plural. This corresponds to the pronouns *er, es, sie* (singular), and *sie* (plural), respectively. The same is true for demonstrative (this, that) and similar adjectives:

| *Masculine* | *Neuter* | *Feminine* | *Plural* | |
|---|---|---|---|---|
| dies*er* | dies*es* | dies*e* | dies*e* | this, these |
| jed*er* | jed*es* | jed*e* | jed*e* | each, every |

The indefinite article *ein,* its negative *kein,* and the possessive adjectives (my, your, his, etc.) have no ending for masculine and neuter singular: *ein, mein, sein, kein, unser, ihr, Ihr*. But in the feminine and plural, they also add the characteristic *-e* ending: *eine, keine, ihre,* etc.

The nominative is also used to complete the verbs *sein, werden,* and *bleiben* (to be, to become, and to remain):

Dieser Mann ist *der Lehrer* — This man is the teacher
Er wurde *ein guter Arzt* — He became a good doctor
Ich bleibe *sein Freund* — I remain his friend

## B) Accusative

The accusative is primarily the case of the direct object (I see *the ball,* he reads *a book,* the man crossed *the street,* etc.). Only masculine words have a distinct accusative form; neuters, feminines, and plurals use the same form for nominative and accusative, for subject and object:

*Das Buch* ist hier — The book is here
Ich lese *das Buch* — I read the book

*Seine Mutter* ist alt — His mother is old
Er liebt *seine Mutter* — He loves his mother

*Die Fenster* sind offen — The windows are open
Ich schliesse *die Fenster* — I close the windows

This is also true for neuter, feminine, and plural pronouns, and for the pronoun you:

*Sie* ist hier — She is here
Ich liebe *sie* — I love *her*

Haben *Sie* eine Zigarette? — Do you have a cigarette?
Ich kann *Sie* nicht verstehen — I can't understand you

*Es* ist spät — It is late
Wollen Sie *es* sehen? — Do you want to see it?

*Sie* sind meine Grosseltern — They are my grandparents
Ich besuche *sie* — I visit them

On the other hand, the characteristic feature of the masculine accusative is the *-n* ending. Here are a few examples:

|  | *Nominative* | *Accusative* |
|---|---|---|
| Pronoun | *er* | ih*n* |
| Definite Article | d*er* | de*n* |
| Indefinite Article | ein | eine*n* |
| Possessive | mein | meine*n* |
| Demonstrative | dies*er* | diese*n* |

The first person pronoun also has accusative forms:

ich — I        wir — we
mich — me      uns — us

The accusative must also be used after certain prepositions. The most important of these are *durch* (through),

*für* (for), *gegen* (against), *ohne* (without), *um* (around).
Examples:

> Er arbeitet für *mich* — He works for me
> Ich kam ohne mein*en* Mantel — I came without my coat
> Wir gehen durch *den* Zug — We walk through the train
> Ich spiele gegen *ihn* — I play against him
> Wir sitzen um *den* Tisch — We sit around the table

## C) Dative

The dative is primarily the case of the indirect object. In English, this function is expressed by the preposition "to," which may either be stated or implied: he gave the man money, or he gave money to the man. In this illustration, "money" is the direct object, and "the man" (or "to the man") is the indirect object. German never uses the preposition "to" to indicate this relationship; instead, we use the dative. The illustrative sentence above would read in German: Er gab *dem Mann* Geld.

The dative has three forms: Masculine and neuter have the characteristic ending *-m,* feminine *-r,* and plural *-n* or *-en.*

|  | *Masculine Neuter* | *Feminine* | *Plural* |
|---|---|---|---|
| Pronoun | ih*m* | ih*r* | ihn*en* |
| Article | de*m* | de*r* | de*n* |
| kein | keine*m* | keine*r* | kcine*n* |
| welches (which) | welche*m* | welche*r* | welche*n* |

The first person pronoun also has a dative form in the singular: ich—mir (I—to me). In the plural, the accusative form *uns* is also used for the dative. Thus, we get the following table for pronouns in all cases:

|  | *Nominative* | *Accusative* | *Dative* |
|---|---|---|---|
| I | ich | mich | mir |
| he | er | ihn | ihm |
| she | sie | sie | ihr |
| it | es | es | ihm |

| | | | |
|---|---|---|---|
| we | wir | uns | uns |
| they | sie | sie | ihnen |
| you (Sing. & Pl.) | Sie | Sie | Ihnen |

All nouns add an *-n* in the dative plural, if it is not already there:

| | *Nominative Singular* | *Nominative Plural* | *Dative Plural* |
|---|---|---|---|
| the man | der Mann | die Männer | den Männer*n* |
| the city | die Stadt | die Städte | den Städte*n* |
| the window | das Fenster | die Fenster | den Fenster*n* |
| the car | der Wagen | die Wagen | den Wagen |
| the woman | die Frau | die Frauen | den Frauen |

A few verbs are always followed by a dative. The most important ones are *antworten* (to answer), *danken* (to thank), *folgen* (to follow), and *helfen* (to help):

> Er antwortet *dem* Lehrer — He answers the teacher
> Ich danke *Ihnen* — I thank you
> Folgen Sie *mir!* — Follow me!
> Können Sie *mir* helfen? — Can you help me?

The dative is also used after certain prepositions. The most important ones are *aus* (out of), *bei* (together with, at), *mit* (with), *nach* (after), *seit* (since), *von* (from), *zu* (to).

*Examples:*

> Er fährt aus *der* Stadt — He drives out of town
> Er wohnt bei *mir* — He lives together with me
> Ich gehe mit *ihm* — I go with him
> Nach *Ihnen!* — After you!
> Seit *diesem* Tag ... — Since that day ...
> Er spricht von *ihr* — He speaks of her
> Wie komme ich zu *dem* Postamt?
>     — How do I get to the postoffice?

Some prepositions, however, can be used with the dative

*or* the accusative. These are *an* (at), *auf* (on), *hinter* (behind), *in* (in), *neben* (next to), *über* (over), *unter* (under), *vor* (before), *zwischen* (between). They are followed by the dative if they show location, the place where something is happening; they are followed by the accusative if they show destination, the place toward which the action is moving. The following examples will illustrate this principle:

> Das Buch ist auf *dem* Tisch
> > — The book is on the table (*Position*)
> Er legt das Buch auf *den* Tisch
> > — He puts the book on the table (*Action*)

> Er steht in *dem* Zimmer
> > — He stands in the room (*Location*)
> Er kommt in *das* Zimmer
> > — He comes into the room (*Direction*)

> Der Ball rollt vor *das* Auto
> > — The ball rolls in front of the car (*Direction*)
> Ein Mann steht vor *dem* anderen
> > — One man stands in front of the other
> > (*Location*)

> Der Hund springt zwischen *das* Bett und *die* Wand
> > — The dog jumps between the bed and the wall
> > (*Action*)
> Der Hund schläft zwischen *dem* Bett und *der* Wand
> > — The dog sleeps between the bed and the wall
> > (*Position*)

Both dative and accusative prepositions may be combined with the article which follows; thus, *in dem* may be shortened to *im, zu der* may become *zur, in das* may be combined as *ins,* etc. These contractions are optional. (Compare English can not—can't.)

*D) Genitive*
The fourth and last German case is the genitive. Occurring

less frequently than the others, it is used to show a relationship between two nouns indicating ownership, belonging together, part and whole, a feature or characteristic, and so on. These are relationships which in English are usually expressed by the preposition "of" (the color of the book, a member of the club, the time of day, etc.) or by a possessive form (Mr. Smith's new house, the teacher's desk). Do not confuse this case with the possessive adjective (*mein, sein, unser,* etc.); an adjective modifies a noun and always has the same case as the noun. Thus, in the sentence "my brother is here," *my* is the subject and therefore nominative: *Mein Bruder ist hier.* In the sentence "I see my brother," *my* is part of the direct object and is therefore accusative: *Ich sehe meinen Bruder.* In the sentence "I show my brother a book," *my* is dative, since it is part of the indirect object (I show the book *to my brother*): *Ich zeige meinem Bruder ein Buch.*

The genitive case, however, as was shown in the examples given above, indicates a relationship *between nouns.* (Pronoun forms of the genitive are becoming obsolete and are hardly ever used any more.) The forms of the genitive are simple: *-es* is the characteristic ending for masculine and neuter, *-er* for feminine and plural. Here is a table of typical forms:

| *Nominative* | *Genitive* |
| --- | --- |
| der, das | des |
| dieser, dieses | dieses |
| ein | eines |
| ihr | ihres |
| die | der |
| jede | jeder |
| alle | aller |

In addition, masculine and neuter nouns also add an *-es* in the genitive singular if they have one syllable, an *-s* if they have more than one syllable. Here are some examples:

die Farbe des Buches — the color of the book
der Sohn dieses Mannes — the son of this man

der neue Hut mein*er* Mutter — my mother's new hat
das Pult d*es* Lehrer*s* — the teacher's desk
der Preis dies*er* Karten — the price of these tickets

For proper names, an *-s* (without apostrophe) is added to show genitive, similar to the English usage:

Karls Schwester — Karl's sister
Frau Schmidts Haus — Mrs. Schmidt's house

As with the other cases, there are some prepositions that are always followed by the genitive. The four most important ones are *anstatt* or *statt* (instead of), *trotz* (in spite of), *während* (during), *wegen* (because of):

(an)statt ein*es* Brief*es* — instead of a letter
trotz d*es* Wetter*s* — in spite of the weather
während d*er* Nacht — during the night
wegen d*es* Regen*s* — because of the rain

## E) *Summary of Case Forms*

|       | *Masculine*                          | *Neuter*              | *Feminine*                                    | *Plural*                                  |
|-------|--------------------------------------|-----------------------|-----------------------------------------------|-------------------------------------------|
| Nom.  | *er*<br>d*er*<br>dies*er*<br>kein    | *es*<br>dies*es*      | sie<br>di*e*                                  |                                           |
| Acc.  | ih*n*<br>d*en*<br>dies*en*<br>kein*en* | das<br>jed*es*<br>kein | sein*e*<br>dies*e*<br>welch*e*               |                                           |
| Dat.  | ih*m*<br>d*em*<br>dies*em*<br>ein*em*<br>jed*em* |       | ih*r*<br>d*er*<br>dies*er*<br>mein*er*<br>unser*er* | ihn*en*<br>d*en*<br>Ihr*en*<br>all*en*<br>welch*en* |

|   | Masculine | Neuter | Feminine | Plural |
|---|---|---|---|---|
|   | *No pronouns* | | | |
| Gen. | des<br>dieses<br>eines<br>unseres | | der<br>jeder<br>keiner<br>seiner | |

Let us now summarize the four German cases and their characteristic endings in one convenient table. Notice that the words *ein, kein,* and the possessives have *no* ending in the masculine nominative and in the neuter nominative/accusative. In all other instances, the pattern is the same for all words, even though only a few typical forms are listed in the table.

Except for the genitive, the first word in each group is the personal pronoun, on which the pattern is based.

## F) *Reflexive and Impersonal Pronouns*

The first person has no reflexive pronoun in German; the regular personal pronouns are used in the accusative and dative:

> Ich wasche mich — I wash (myself)
> Ich kaufte mir einen Hut — I bought myself a hat
> Wir unterhielten uns — We enjoyed ourselves

For all other forms, accusative or dative, singular and plural (yourself, yourselves, himself, herself, itself, themselves), the word *sich* is used:

> Er rasiert sich — He shaves (himself)
> Sie kauft sich ein Kleid — She buys herself a dress
> Haben Sie sich geschnitten? — Did you cut yourself?
> Die Kinder versteckten sich
>    — The children hid (themselves)

As some of the above examples show, German often uses the reflexive when English does not need to.

German frequently uses the impersonal pronoun *man*. It means "one," "we," "you," "they," "people," "someone," "everyone," "anyone," or whatever else fits the English sentence. It does *not* mean "man." It occurs only in the nominative and is always the subject of its sentence.

> Hier spricht man Englisch
> — Here one speaks English (someone speaks English, English is spoken, etc.)
> Wo kann man Äpfel kaufen?
> — Where can one (I, we, you) buy apples?
> Man weiss nie, was man braucht
> — One never knows what one needs
> (You never know what you need)

# 5. *Adjectives and Adverbs*

German adjectives that precede a noun always have the same case as the noun that they modify and must have a case ending.

On the other hand, adjectives have no ending when they are in the predicate, *i.e.* when they complete the verbs *sein* (to be), *werden* (to become or get), and *bleiben* (to remain), without a noun following. For example:

> Sie ist krank — She is sick
> Es wird spät — It is getting late
> Er ist dumm und bleibt dumm
> — He is stupid and remains (will remain) stupid

Adverbs formed from adjectives also have no endings:

> Sie ist schön — She is beautiful
> Sie singt schön — She sings beautifully
>
> Das Wetter wird kalt — The weather is getting cold
> Er spricht kalt — He speaks coldly

Most adjectives, however, are followed by a noun and must have an ending. The basic principle governing these endings is not complicated: if there has not been any ending *before* the descriptive adjective, the adjective itself takes the characteristic (or primary) ending for that particular case, as indicated in the table of endings for articles, pronouns, etc. For instance:

Kalt*es* Wasser ist gut (*Nom. Ntr.*)
  — Cold water is good
Kalt*er* Kaffee ist gut (*Nom. Masc.*)
  — Cold coffee is good
Sie hat schön*e* Hände (*Acc. Pl.*)
  — She has beautiful hands
Er arbeitet mit gross*em* Eifer (*Dat. Masc.* because of *mit*)
  — He works with great zeal

After *ein, kein, mein, sein, ihr,* etc., which have no ending (as we have seen in the table), the adjective itself must take the ending *-er* if the following noun is masculine, *-es* if it is neuter: ein alt*er* Mann (an old man), ein alt*es* Buch (an old book).

Thus, the full range of primary endings will be added to the adjective, if these endings have not already occurred previously. If, however, the primary ending is found on a word preceding the descriptive adjective (an article, possessive, demonstrative, etc.), then the adjective carries one of two possible secondary endings: *-e* for all nominative singulars and the accusative singular feminine and neuter. For example, der alt*e* Mann (the old man), die alt*e* Frau (the old woman), das alt*e* Buch (the old book). Notice that in these instances the article has already indicated that the following noun is masculine, feminine, or neuter. Therefore the descriptive adjective no longer makes any distinction.

In all other cases, including all plurals, the secondary ending is *-en:*

Ich sehe den alt*en* Lehrer — I see the old teacher
mit meiner alt*en* Mutter — with my old mother

die Farbe des alt*en* Buches — the color of the old book
alle meine alt*en* Freunde — all my old friends

Let us state the principle again: If the primary ending has
not occurred *before* the descriptive adjective, we put it *on*
the descriptive adjective. If it has occurred before, the descriptive adjective has the secondary ending -*e* or -*en*.

Descriptive adjectives in a series all have the same ending:
ein arm*er*, alt*er*, krank*er* Mann (a poor, old, sick man);
alle meine lieb*en* alt*en* Freunde (all my dear old friends).

In English, adjectives are sometimes used as nouns, in expressions such as "the rich and the poor," "the old and the
new." This also happens in German. In this case, the adjective is capitalized and its ending remains the same as it
would have been if the noun were there. Thus "a sick man"
is *ein kranker Mann* or simply *ein Kranker.* "A sick woman"
is *eine kranke Frau*, or just *eine Kranke.* Konrad Adenauer's
nickname in Germany is *"der Alte"* (the old man).

*Comparison*
There are three levels of comparison: the positive (normal
form), the comparative, and the superlative. When we compare two things that are on the same level, such as "He is as
old as I," we say in German "Er ist *so* alt *wie* ich."

The comparative is formed by adding the ending -*er* to
the German adjective. Most one-syllable adjectives also take
an *Umlaut:* alt—älter (old—older); jung—jünger (young
—younger); gross—grösser (big—bigger).

This ending is used for all adjectives, no matter how long
they may be: interessant—interessant*er* (interesting—more
interesting). Adverbs also form their comparative in the
same way: Sprechen Sie langsam! (Speak slowly!) —
Sprechen Sie langsam*er!* (Speak more slowly!)

When comparing two things on different levels, such as
"He is older than I," we say in German: "Er ist älter *als* ich."

The superlative is formed by adding the ending -*st* to
the stem of the adjective, again with an *Umlaut* for most
one-syllable adjectives: der schön*ste* (the most beautiful),

die jüng*ste* (the youngest), das interessant*este* (the most interesting).

Adverbs have a slightly different superlative form. We use the preposition *am* and add the ending *-sten:*

>  Sie singt *am* schön*sten* — She sings most beautifully
>  Er spricht *am* schnell*sten* — He speaks most rapidly

A few adjectives and adverbs have irregular comparatives and superlatives, as in English:

>  gut—besser—der beste (am besten)
>  good—better—best
>  viel—mehr—am meisten
>  much—more—most

Adjectives in the comparative and superlative take the regular endings, depending on the noun that they modify:

>  meine jünger*e* Schwester — my younger sister
>  mit meiner jünger*en* Schwester — with my younger sister
>  mein ältest*er* Bruder — my oldest brother
>  mein schwerst*es* Buch — my most difficult book
>  das schwerst*e* Buch — the most difficult book

## 6. *Word Order*

Before discussing some special verb forms, let us turn our attention to what we have called the second critical problem of German grammar, that of word order. We have already learned two important rules:

1) If the subject does not come at the beginning of the sentence, it will come immediately after the verb. Thus, for example:

>  Heute sprechen wir Deutsch
>      — Today we are speaking German

Zeigen Sie mir das Buch!
— Show me the book!
Gehen wir heute ins Kino?
— Are we going to the movies today?


2) Not all of the German verb is found in one place. If a clause contains more than one verb form, the completion of the verbal idea will be placed at the end of the clause. For example, *spazieren gehen* means "to go walking." We say in German:


Ich gehe spazieren — I go walking
Ich gehe oft spazieren — I often go walking
Ich gehe oft im Park spazieren
— I often go walking in the park
Ich gehe oft mit meinen Freunden im Park spazieren
— I often go walking in the park with my friends
Ich gehe oft im Sommer mit meinen Freunden im Park spazieren
— I often go walking in the park with my friends in summer


And so on. Notice that the phrase "go walking" is always a unit in English, but that it gets split apart farther and farther in German.

We can summarize both rules in one formula, where (as we have done it before) S stands for the subject, O for the object, $V_1$ the first part of the verb, $V_2$ the second part of the verb, and x any element other than the subject): The German sentence structure follows either the pattern S — $V_1$ — O ———— $V_2$ or x — $V_1$ — S — O ———— $V_2$. $V_2$, the second part of the verb, can have various forms. It can be a so-called separable prefix, as in *auf*stehen (to get up):


Ich stehe um sechs Uhr *auf* — I get up at six o'clock

It can be a past participle, such as:

> Ich habe viele gute Bücher *gelesen*
> — I have read many good books

It can be an infinitive, such as:

> Können Sie mir bitte ein Glas Wasser *bringen?*
> — Can you please bring me a glass of water?

Now some other important word order rules. First, the sequence of direct and indirect object, as in the last example above: The direct *pronoun* object comes before the indirect object, but the direct *noun* object comes after the indirect object. Thus,

> Ich gebe dem Mann das Buch — I give the man the book
> Ich gebe ihm das Buch — I give him the book
> Ich gebe es dem Mann — I give it to the man
> Ich gebe es ihm — I give it to him

Notice that English follows an identical sequence.

Adverbs and prepositional phrases (here, now, in my house, after school, etc.) have a very definite sequence in German. The usual order is Time — Manner — Place or, to put it differently, you answer the questions when?, how? (or why?), where? in that order. While in English we say "He is here today," in German we say "Er ist heute hier." Take the sentence "We went to Europe by boat last summer." In German, the sentence would read as follows: *Wir fuhren letzten Sommer* (Time, when?) *auf einem Schiff* (Manner, how?) *nach Europa.* (Place, where?) Or take the sentence "He came home drunk yesterday." In German, we would say: *Er kam gestern betrunken nach Hause*.

The sequence will be altered only very rarely and in special circumstances. By and large, most Germans follow it instinctively (although they would be hard put to tell you why), and you had best follow it, too.

The word *nicht* is an adverb of negation and is considered in German as an adverb of manner. It will therefore follow expressions of time and precede expressions of place:

> Sie ist heute nicht hier — She is not here today

Our expanded sentence diagram now reads as follows: (DPO — direct pronoun object; IO — indirect object; DNO — direct noun object; T — time; M — manner; P — place)

$$S - V_1 - DPO - IO - DNO - T - M - P - V_2 \text{ or}$$
$$x - V_1 - S - DPO \text{———} V_2$$

Of course, no sentence will contain all of these elements — but the ones that are there should be in this sequence.

Occasionally, an adverb of time may precede a noun object. This happens especially if the adverb of time would otherwise come at the end of the sentence, a position that German avoids if at all possible. For example:

> Ich habe diesen Film gestern gesehen
> — I've seen this film yesterday
> Ich sah gestern einen guten Film
> — I saw a good movie yesterday
> Er liest jetzt die Zeitung
> — He's reading the paper now

Of course, the problem can be avoided simply by putting the adverb of time at the beginning of the sentence:

> Gestern sah ich einen guten Film
> — Yesterday I saw a good movie
> Jetzt liest er die Zeitung
> — Now he's reading the paper

But note the position of the subject in these sentences.


*Dependent Clauses*
Up to now we have concerned ourselves only with word

order problems in a main or independent clause. In a dependent clause, there is a fundamental change: the first part of the verb ($V_1$) moves from its normal position *to the very end of the clause,* after the second part of the verb ($V_2$), if there is one. A simplified diagram of the dependent clause looks like this:

$$\left.\begin{array}{l} \text{conjunction} \\ \text{relative} \end{array}\right\} \quad \text{— S — O — } \ldots \text{ — } V_2 \text{ — } V_1$$

Dependent clauses are introduced either by a conjunction (conj.) or by a relative pronoun (rel.).

*A) Conjunctions*
There are two types of conjunctions: coordinating and subordinating. Coordinating conjunctions join two words, phrases, clauses, or sentences of equal significance and do not affect word order at all. The five important coordinating conjunctions in German are *und* (and), *aber* (but), *sondern* (but on the contrary, but rather), *oder* (or), and *denn* (for):

Ich kam und ich sprach mit ihm
   — I came and I talked with him
Ich kam, aber er war nicht da
   — I came, but he was not there
Das Wasser ist nicht kalt, sondern es ist warm
   — The water is not cold, but on the contrary it is warm
Ich muss gehen, denn es ist spät
   — I must go, for it is late

A subordinating conjunction introduces a dependent clause, in which the verb comes at the end. The most important subordinating conjunctions are

| | |
|---|---|
| als — when | ob — whether |
| bevor — before | obgleich ⎱ — although |
| bis — until | obwohl ⎰ |
| da — since (reason) | seit, seitdem — since (time) |
| damit — so that | während — while |

| | |
|---|---|
| dass — that | weil — because |
| nachdem — after | wenn — if, whenever |

Here are a few examples:

> Ich muss gehen, weil es schon spät ist
> > — I have to go, because it is already late
>
> Er wartete, bis sein Freund nach Hause kam
> > — He waited until his friend came home
>
> Ich muss viel studieren, damit ich gut Deutsch
> sprechen kann
> > — I have to study a lot, so that
> > I can speak German well
>
> Ich weiss nicht, ob ich dieses Buch gan
> verstanden habe
> > — I don't know whether I have understood
> > this book completely
>
> Ich glaube, dass er heute Abend kommen wird
> > — I believe that he will come tonight

Interrogatives can also be used as conjunctions. The most important interrogatives are listed below:

| | |
|---|---|
| wer? — who? | wann? — when? |
| wen? (Acc.) — whom? | warum? — why? |
| wem? (Dat.) — to whom? | wie? — how? |
| wessen? (Gen.) — whose? | wo? — where? |
| welcher? — which? | wohin? — where to? |
| was? — what? | woher? — where from? |

Here are some examples of their use to introduce dependent clauses:

> Wissen Sie, wann die Kinder von der Schule
> zurückkommen?
> > — Do you know when the children
> > come back from school?
>
> Er fragte mich, mit wem ich gestern Abend
> gesprochen hatte
> > — He asked me with whom I had spoken last night

Er wollte wissen, warum ich Deutsch studiere
  — He wanted to know why I am studying German
Ich weiss noch nicht, wohin wir heute Nachmittag
 gehen werden
   — I don't know yet where we will
    go (to) this afternoon

If the sentence begins with the dependent clause (and therefore not with the subject), the subject of the main clause must come after the verb:

Wenn er uns besuchen kommt, werde ich mit
 ihm sprechen
  — If he comes to visit us, I will talk to him
Weil es heute regnet, bleiben wir zu Hause
  — Because it is raining today, we are staying home

In other words, if the main clause comes second, its subject comes second.

The conjunction *dass* (that) is sometimes omitted. In that case, normal word order is used:

Er sagt, dass er krank ist — He says that he is sick
Er sagt, er ist krank — He says he is sick

The conjunction *wenn* (if) is also sometimes omitted. In that case, the verb is placed at the beginning of the sentence, the subject comes next, and the second clause usually begins with the word *so* (then):

Regnet es, so bleiben wir zu Hause
  —If it rains, (then) we stay home

Compare the English sentence: Had I the money, I would buy a car. Although the construction occurs more frequently in German than it does in English, it is mainly found in literature and is fairly rare in colloquial speech.

*B) Relative Pronouns*
A dependent clause can also begin with a relative pronoun

(who, which, that, etc.). In English, these are for the most part identical with the interrogatives "who," "which," and so forth. In German, this is not the case. Basically, the German relative pronoun uses the definite article, although in some cases a slightly longer form must be used. The gender and number of a relative pronoun must be identical with the noun to which it refers:

> der Mann, der ... — the man who . . .
> die Frau, die ... — the woman who . . .
> das Kind, das ... — the child who . . .
> meine Freunde, die ... — my friends who . . .

This also applies to inanimate objects:

> der Tisch, der ... — the table which . . .
> das Buch, das ... — the book that . . .
> die Häuser, die ... — the houses which . . .

The case of the relative pronoun depends on its use in the sentence. Here is a complete list:

|      | *Masculine* | *Neuter* | *Feminine* | *Plural* |
|------|------------|----------|------------|----------|
| Nom. | der        | das      | die        |          |
| Acc. | den        | das      | die        |          |
| Dat. | dem        | dem      | der        | *denen*  |
| Gen. | *dessen*   | *dessen* | *deren*    | *deren*  |

The words in italics identify those forms which are not quite identical with the article: the dative plural *denen,* the genitive masculine or neuter *dessen,* and the genitive feminine or plural *deren.* The following examples show the four cases for the masculine only. The other genders and the plural use their forms correspondingly:

Der Mann, *der* dort sitzt, ist mein Bruder
— The man who sits there is my brother
Der Mann, *den* Sie dort sehen, ist mein Bruder
— The man whom you see there is my brother
Der Mann, mit *dem* ich sprach, ist mein Bruder
— The man with whom I spoke is my brother
Der Mann, *dessen* Haus Sie dort sehen, ist mein Bruder
— The man, whose house you see there, is my brother

Unlike English, German *never* omits the relative pronoun.


# 7. *The Passive Voice*

As in English, the German passive shows an action that the subject does not perform, but that is happening to the subject. "The man writes the letter" is active. "The letter was written by the man" is passive. A passive sentence therefore has four basic elements: the subject (*the letter*), the helping verb (*was*), the past participle of the main verb (*written*), and the agent who actually performs the action (*the man*).

These same four elements also occur in the German passive, although not in the same sequence. The subject, as always, is in the nominative. Hence, in our model sentence, *der Mann*. The German helping verb is not the verb to be, as in English, but rather the verb *werden*, which must be used in the corresponding tense. Since our model used the past tense (*was*), we must use the past tense of *werden*, *wurde: Der Brief wurde*. ... The past participle, as always in the German sentence, appears at the end: *Der Brief wurde ... geschrieben*. Finally, we insert the agent, for which German uses the preposition *von* and the dative; in our case, *von dem Mann*. The whole sentence thus reads:

*Der Brief wurde von dem Mann geschrieben.*

This sentence is of course possible in all tenses:

Present: Der Brief *wird* von dem Mann geschrieben.
Past: Der Brief *wurde* von dem Mann geschrieben.
Perfect: Der Brief *ist* von dem Mann geschrieben *worden*.
Future: Der Brief *wird* von dem Mann geschrieben *werden*.

Notice that nothing changes except the form of *werden:*
For the present, we use *ich werde* and *er wird* in the singular, *werden* in the plural. In the past, we have *wurde* in the singular and *wurden* in the plural. For the perfect, we use *ist ... worden* in the singular, *sind ... worden* in the plural, to correspond to English has or have been. In the future, *werden* is used twice: *wird ... werden* for English will be.

As you can see, the verb *werden* is very important in German. In fact, it has three completely different functions. These can be identified not by the form of the verb itself, but by the other words that complete the verbal unit. These, however, will be found at the end of the sentence or clause. When *werden* is used with a noun or an adjective, it means "to get," "grow," "turn" or "become":

Die Blätter werden braun — The leaves get (turn) brown
Es wurde spät — It got (became) late
Er ist mein Freund geworden — He has become my friend

When it is used with an infinitive, it indicates future:

Ich werde gehen — I shall (will) go
Er wird mit Ihnen sprechen — He will talk to you

Finally, when it is used together with a past participle, it indicates the passive, as we have seen above:

Der Brief wurde geschrieben — The letter was written

Thus, the meaning of *werden* depends on the word with which it is associated. Remember, however, that this word need not follow the verb *werden* immediately; it usually comes at the end of the sentence and may be quite far removed. You can not know the meaning of *werden* until you look at the end of the sentence or clause. But as we have told you, this is a very good habit to form anyway: always look to the end of the sentence to finish the verbal idea.

One more thing about the passive: When the agent is not expressed or is unknown, German often avoids the passive altogether and uses the indefinite pronoun *man* instead:

> Das tut man nicht — One does not do that, you don't
>    do that, people don't do that, that is not done
> Man hat einen Brief geschrieben
>    — Someone wrote a letter, a letter was written

## 8. The Subjunctive

The main use for the subjunctive in German is to indicate conditions that are contrary to fact: If he were here, he would help me. This obviously means that he is not here. I am only talking about what might happen if he came.

Let us first look at the forms of the subjunctive, and then examine its use. Regular verbs have no subjunctive, they just use the past tense, as in English:

> Wenn Napoleon heute lebte, ...
>    — If Napoleon lived today ...

Irregular verbs add an -*e* to the singular of the past tense, (if it is not already there), and an *Umlaut* on the stem vowel (if possible, and if it isn't already there):

> Wenn ich hätte ... — If I had ...
> Wenn er wäre ... — If he were ...
> Wenn Sie kämen ... — If you came ...
> Wenn wir könnten ... — If we could ...
> Wenn sie ginge ... — If she went ...

This part of the statement is called "the condition." It is followed by the conclusion, which contains the word *würde* (would) and the infinitive. Thus, the sentence "If he were here, he would help me" reads in German:

> Wenn er hier wäre, würde er mir helfen.

We can also turn it around ("He would help me if he were here"):

> Er würde mir helfen, wenn er hier wäre.

Sometimes, especially with *sein, haben,* and the modals, *würde* is left out, and the subjunctive is used in both halves of the sentence:

> Wenn er käme, wäre ich froh
> — If he came, I would be glad
> Ich könnte es tun, wenn ich wollte
> — I could do it if I wanted

When we are referring to a past condition, the situation is even more unreal: If he had come, he would have helped me. This is sheer hypothesis, since he obviously did not come and thus could not help me. I am merely expressing my idea of what would have happened if he had been there. In this type of sentence, German just uses *hätte* or *wäre* (would have) plus the past participle of the verb. (Remember that some verbs must use the helping verb *sein* instead of *haben*.) The above sentence therefore reads in German:

> Wenn er gekommen wäre, hätte er mir geholfen.

Or, by inverting the two clauses:

> Er hätte mir geholfen, wenn er gekommen wäre.

German also uses the subjunctive for indirect quotation, to indicate that you are not sure whether the statement you attribute to somebody else is really true. Take, for example, the sentence "He said he was sick." Since you do not know whether he is telling the truth, you say in German "Er sagte, er *wäre* krank," which implies something like "He claims to be sick." This form, however, is primarily found in literature. Many Germans do not use it in everyday conversation, and you'll manage to get by without it. When you do encounter it, either in speaking or in writing, you should not have too much trouble identifying and understanding it.

# 9. Familiar Form

Finally, a few words about the familiar or intimate form of the second person. Up to now, we have learned only one word for "you," both singular and plural: *Sie,* which is used with the plural (infinitive) form of the verb.

There are, however, two other forms, which are used for family, close friends, small children, animals, and in prayer. They are *du* in the singular and *ihr* in the plural. In all tenses, the verb with *du* ends in *-st,* and with *ihr* in *-t* (except for the present tense of the verb *sein*). If the stem ends in a *-d* or *-t,* a linking *-e-* is inserted before the ending:

| | | |
|---|---|---|
| sein (to be) | du bist | ihr seid |
| haben (to have) | du hast | ihr habt |
| finden (to find) | du findest | ihr findet |
| gehen (to go) | du gehst | ihr geht |
| kommen (to come) (PAST) | du kamst | ihr kamt |

Some verbs have a vowel change in the present tense. It occurs only in the singular and is the same as that for the third person:

| | | |
|---|---|---|
| werden (to become) | du wirst | ihr werdet |
| können (can) | du kannst | ihr könnt |
| fahren (to drive) | du fährst | ihr fahrt |
| geben (to give) | du gibst | ihr gebt |
| lesen (to read) | du liest | ihr lest |

The imperative of this form usually consists of the stem only, although some verbs change from *e* to *i* or *ie:*

> Komm hier! — Come here!
> Bring mir ... — Bring me ...
> Gib mir ... — Give me ...
> Zeig mir ... — Show me ...
> Lauf nicht! — Don't run!
> Lies das Buch! — Read the book!
> Sprich langsamer! — Speak more slowly!

The forms *du* and *ihr* also have other cases. The accusative of *du* is *dich,* the dative *dir.* Dative and accusative of *ihr* is *euch.* There are no distinct reflexive pronouns; *dich, dir,* and *euch* are used reflexively as well.

The possessive adjective (your) for *du* is *dein,* that for *ihr* is *euer:*

> Marie, ist das dein Hut?
> > — Marie, is that your hat?
> Ich sah dich mit dein*em* Bruder
> > — I saw you with your brother
> Kinder, wascht euer*e* Hände
> > — Children, wash your hands

As you see, regular adjective endings may be added to these forms.

Unless you have relatives in Germany, you are not likely to use these forms very often. To say *du* to somebody indicates a considerable degree of intimacy, or close relationship. The average adult German has only a handful of really good friends, outside of his family, to whom he says *du.* A general rule of thumb might be to use *du* when you are on a first-name basis (which doesn't happen in Germany so often and as quickly as it does in America), and to use *Sie* with the last name, when you say *Herr, Frau,* or *Fräulein,* and certainly to strangers. An even simpler rule of thumb is this: When in doubt, use *Sie.* It is not only easier, but it will get you into less trouble. It is always better to say *Sie* to a little boy than to say *du* to a German policeman.

## Summary

What we have given you are not *all* the rules of German grammar. As is the case with any language, there are many complications and exceptions, there are rules for the exceptions and exceptions from the rules. This book only gives you the basic principles. But if you learn these, study the vocabulary, and work with the pictures in the book, you will go a long way.

# Pictorial Section

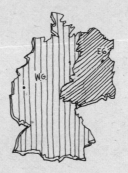

Hier ist Deutschland.

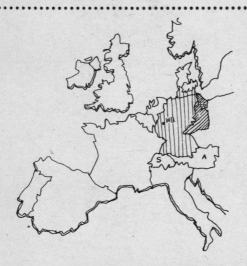

Deutschland ist in Europa.

Hier ist Westdeutschland    und hier ist Ostdeutschland.

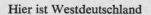

Hier ist Berlin.
Berlin ist in Ostdeutschland.

Deutschland ist ein Land in Europa.

Berlin ist eine Stadt
in Deutschland.
Berlin ist die Hauptstadt
von Ostdeutschland.

Bonn ist eine Stadt
in Deutschland.
Bonn ist die Hauptstadt
von Westdeutschland.

Hier ist Österreich.
Österreich ist ein
Land in Europa.

Hier ist Wien.
Wien ist eine Stadt
in Österreich.
Wien ist die Hauptstadt
von Österreich.

Hier ist die Schweiz.
Die Schweiz ist ein
Land in Europa.

Hier ist Zürich.
Zürich ist eine Stadt
in der Schweiz.

Deutschland, Österreich und die Schweiz sind in Europa.
Deutschland, Österreich und die Schweiz sind Länder
in Europa. In Deutschland, in Österreich und in der
Schweiz sprechen wir Deutsch.

Hier ist England.     Hier ist Amerika.

In England und in Amerika sprechen wir Englisch.

Hier ist ein Deutscher.
Er spricht Deutsch.

Hier ist ein Österreicher.
Er spricht Deutsch.

Hier ist ein Schweizer.
Er spricht Deutsch.

Hier ist ein Deutscher,
ein Österreicher und
ein Schweizer.
Sie sprechen Deutsch.

72

Hier ist ein Engländer.
Er spricht Englisch.

Hier ist ein Amerikaner.
Er spricht Englisch.

Sprechen Sie Deutsch?
Nein, wir sprechen Englisch.

Hier ist ein Engländer
und ein Amerikaner.
Sie sprechen Englisch.

Ich bin ein Mann.
Ich bin ein Deutscher.
Ich spreche Deutsch.

Ich bin Wilhelm Schmidt.
Mein Name ist Wilhelm
Schmidt. Ich heisse
Wilhelm Schmidt.

Ich bin eine Frau.
Ich bin eine Deutsche.
Ich spreche Deutsch.

Ich bin Anna Schmidt.
Mein Name ist Anna Schmidt.
Ich heisse Anna Schmidt.

Anna ist meine Frau.
Sie ist meine Frau.
Sie ist Frau Schmidt.

Wilhelm ist mein Mann.
Er ist mein Mann.
Er ist Herr Schmidt.

Wir sind Mann und Frau.
Wir sind Herr und Frau
Schmidt. Wir sind Deutsche.

Das ist die Familie
Schmidt. Wir sind eine
deutsche Familie.

Das sind meine Kinder.
Wir haben drei Kinder.

Das ist Fräulein Schmidt.
Sie heisst Gretchen.
Gretchen ist meine Tochter.

Das ist mein Sohn Otto.
Er heisst Otto.

Und das ist mein Sohn
Karl. Er heisst Karl.

Gretchen, Karl und Otto
sind die Kinder.

Herr und Frau Schmidt
sind die Eltern.

Karl und Otto sind unsere
Söhne. Wir haben zwei Söhne.
Wir haben zwei Söhne
und eine Tochter.

Wir sind fünf Personen
in unserer Familie. Eins,
zwei, drei, vier, fünf.

Hier ist der Grossvater

und hier ist die Grossmutter.

Die Grossmutter und der
Grossvater sind die
Grosseltern.
Sie sind die Grosseltern.

Die Grosseltern sind alt.
Die Kinder sind jung.

Otto ist mein Bruder.
Er ist zehn Jahre alt.

Otto ist jung.
Er ist jünger als ich.

Karl ist mein Bruder.
Er ist 13 (dreizehn)
Jahre alt.

Er ist jünger als ich,
aber älter als Otto.
Otto ist der jüngste.

Gretchen ist meine
Schwester. Sie ist 19
(neunzehn) Jahre alt.

Gretchen ist älter als ich.
Sie ist älter als mein
Bruder. Sie ist
älter als wir.

Karl ist älter als ich.
Gretchen ist am ältesten.

Sie ist das älteste
Kind in unserer Familie.

Wer ist das?
Das ist Herr Müller.
Er ist unser Freund.

Wer ist das?
Das ist die Müller
Familie. Wir sind
Freunde. Sie sind
unsere Freunde.

Ich heisse Müller.
Wie heissen Sie?
Wer sind Sie?

Ich heisse Schultz.
Ich bin Herr Schultz.
Und wie heissen Sie?
Sind Sie Herr Müller?
Ja, ich bin Herr Müller.

Bin ich ein Mann?
Ja, ich bin ein Mann.

Ist das ein Mann?
Nein, das ist kein Mann,
das ist eine Frau.
Das ist Frau Schmidt.

Wer ist das? Ist das
eine Frau?
Nein, das ist keine Frau,
das ist ein Mädchen.
Das ist Gretchen.
Sie ist ein Mädchen.

Ist das ein Mädchen?
Nein, das ist kein
Mädchen, das ist ein Junge.
Karl ist ein Junge.
Karl und Otto sind Jungen.

Was ist das? Das ist
eine Katze. Unsere Katze
heisst Mimi.

Und hier ist unser Hund.
Er ist ein Dachshund.
Er heisst Fritz.

Die Müller Familie hat
keine Katze. Sie haben
keinen Hund. Sie haben
einen Vogel.

Hier ist ihr Vogel.
Er ist ein Kanarienvogel.
Er heisst Hansi.

Was ist das? Das ist
ein Haus.
Das ist
unser Haus.

Hier ist eine Strasse.
Hier sind Häuser.
Eine Strasse hat viele
Häuser.

Unser Haus ist in dieser
Strasse. Wir wohnen hier.
Wir wohnen in diesem Haus.

Ich wohne hier, meine
Frau wohnt hier und meine
Kinder wohnen hier. Wir
alle wohnen in
diesem Haus.

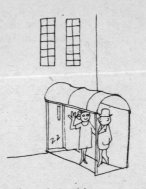

Herr und Frau Müller
wohnen nicht in unserer
Strasse. Sie wohnen in
diesem Haus.

Sie wohnen hier.
Sie haben eine Wohnung
in diesem Haus.

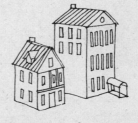

Unser Haus ist klein.
Unser Haus ist nicht so
gross wie dieses Haus.

Unser Haus ist kleiner
als dieses Haus.
Dieses Haus ist grösser
als unser Haus.

Hier ist ein Zimmer in
unserem Haus.
Es ist das Wohnzimmer.

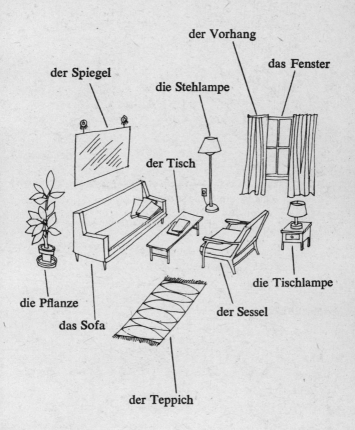

der Vorhang

das Fenster

der Spiegel

die Stehlampe

der Tisch

die Pflanze

das Sofa

die Tischlampe

der Sessel

der Teppich

Hier ist das Speisezimmer.

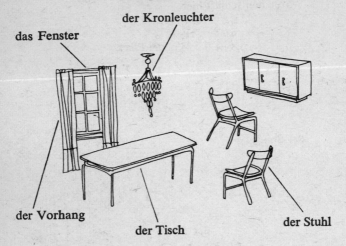

der Kronleuchter

das Fenster

der Vorhang

der Tisch

der Stuhl

Das ist ein Schlafzimmer.
Vater und Mutter
schlafen hier.

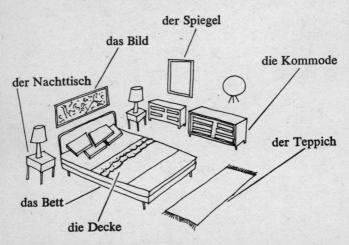

der Spiegel

das Bild

die Kommode

der Nachttisch

das Bett

die Decke

der Teppich

Das ist Gretchens Zimmer.
Gretchen schläft hier.

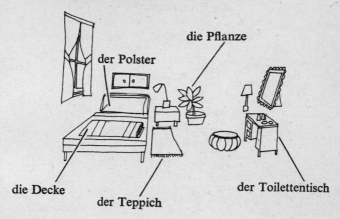

die Pflanze

der Polster

die Decke

der Teppich

der Toilettentisch

Und hier schlafen
Karl und Otto.

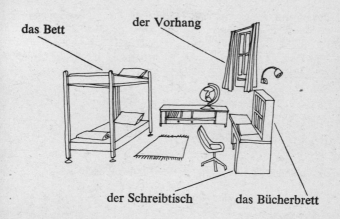

das Bett

der Vorhang

der Schreibtisch

das Bücherbrett

## Das ist die Küche.

der Küchenschrank     der Spültisch

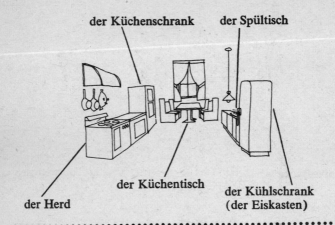

der Küchentisch

der Herd           der Kühlschrank
(der Eiskasten)

## Hier ist unser Badezimmer.

die Brause       das Handtuch       der Spiegel

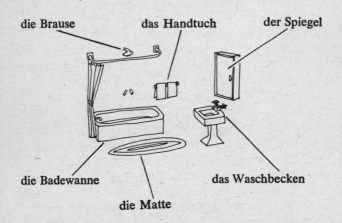

die Badewanne           das Waschbecken

die Matte

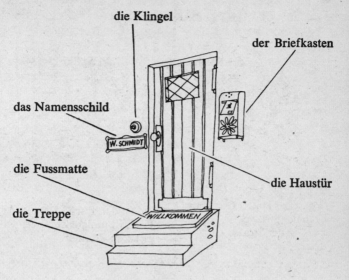

die Klingel

der Briefkasten

das Namensschild

W. SCHMIDT

die Haustür

die Fussmatte

die Treppe

WILLKOMMEN

Hier ist unser Haus.
Unser Haus ist nicht gross.
Unser Haus ist klein.

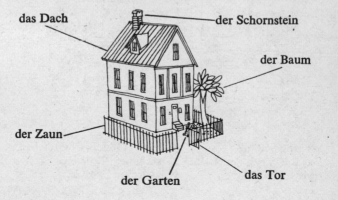

das Dach

der Schornstein

der Baum

der Zaun

der Garten

das Tor

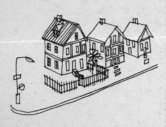

Wo ist das Haus? Das Haus
ist in der Strasse.
Es ist in der Strasse.

Wo ist der Tisch? Der
Tisch ist in dem Zimmer.
Er ist im Zimmer.

Wo ist das Bild?
Das Bild ist an der Wand.
Es ist an der Wand.

Wo ist Gretchen? Gretchen
ist an dem Fenster.
Sie ist am Fenster.

Wo ist das Glas? Das Glas
ist auf dem Tisch.
Es ist auf dem Tisch.

Wo ist Fritz?
Fritz ist auf dem Bett.
Er schläft.

Wo ist Mimi? Mimi ist
unter dem Tisch.
Sie schläft auch.

Wo sind die Stühle? Die
Stühle sind um den Tisch.
Sie sind um den Tisch.

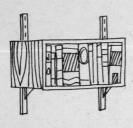

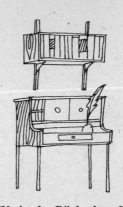

Wo sind die Bücher?
Die Bücher sind auf dem
Bücherbrett. Sie sind auf
dem Bücherbrett.

Wo ist das Bücherbrett?
Das Bücherbrett ist über
dem Schreibtisch. Es ist
über dem Schreibtisch.

Wo ist das grosse Buch?
Wo ist dieses Buch? Es ist
zwischen den zwei
kleinen Büchern.

Wo ist die Lampe?
Sie ist zwischen dem
Sofa und dem Sessel.
Die Lampe ist zwischen
dem Sofa und dem Sessel.

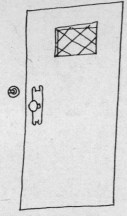

Wo ist die Klingel?
Die Klingel ist neben der
Tür. Sie ist neben der Tür.

Wo sind die Gläser?
Die Gläser sind auf dem
Küchentisch. Sie sind auf
dem Küchentisch.

Das kleine Glas ist vor
dem grossen Glas.

Das grosse Glas ist hinter
dem kleinen Glas.

Wo ist Herr Schmidt? Was
tut er?
Er kommt in das Zimmer.
Er kommt ins Zimmer.

Er kommt durch die Tür.

Er geht zu dem Fenster.

Er geht von der Tür
zum Fenster.

Er sieht durch das
Fenster.

Er sieht in den Garten.

Er sieht aus dem
Fenster in den Garten.

Er geht zu der (zur) Tür.
Er geht von dem (vom)
Fenster zur Tür.

Herr Schmidt hat ein
Buch in der Hand.

Er geht mit dem Buch zu
dem (zum) Bücherbrett.

Er stellt das Buch auf
das Bücherbrett. Das Buch
ist auf dem Bücherbrett.

Er kommt ohne das Buch
zurück. Er hat das
Buch nicht.

1. Was ist das?

2. Was ist das?

3. Was ist das?

4. Was ist das?

5. Was ist das?

6. Wer ist das?

7. Wer ist das?

8. Wer ist das?

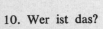

9. Wer ist das?

10. Wer ist das?

11. Was ist das?

12. Was ist das?

13. Was ist das?

14. Was ist das?

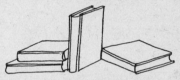

15. Was ist das?

16. Wo ist Deutschland?

17. Wo ist der Spiegel?

18. Wo ist der Kronleuchter?

19. Wo ist Gretchen?

20. Wo sind die Bücher?

21. Was tut Frau Schmidt?

22. Was tut Karl?

23. Was tut Otto?

24. Was tut Gretchen?

25. Was tut Mimi?

### ANSWERS

1. Das ist ein Haus.
2. Das sind Häuser.
3. Das ist ein Hund.
4. Das ist eine Katze.
5. Das ist ein Vogel.
6. Das ist ein Mann. Das ist Herr Schmidt.
7. Das ist eine Frau. Das ist Frau Schmidt.
8. Das ist ein Mädchen. Das ist Gretchen.
9. Das ist ein Junge. Das ist Karl.
10. Das sind Kinder.
11. Das ist ein Tisch.
12. Das sind zwei Stühle.
13. Das sind vier Bücher.
14. Das ist eine Tür.
15. Das ist ein Fenster.
16. Deutschland ist in Europa.
17. Der Spiegel ist an der Wand.
    Er ist an der Wand.
18. Der Kronleuchter ist über dem Tisch.
    Er ist über dem Tisch.
19. Sie ist zwischen Karl und Otto.
20. Sie sind auf dem Schreibtisch.
21. Sie kommt durch die Tür.
22. Er geht zum Fenster.
23. Er sieht durch das Fenster.
24. Sie geht aus dem Haus.
25. Sie schläft unter dem Stuhl.

das Auge

das Haar

die Zähne

der Kopf

das Ohr

die Hand

die Nase

die Lippen

die Zunge

der Mund

das Ohr

der Kopf

die Nase

das Haar

das Auge

die Finger

der rechte Arm

der Mund

der Hals

der Körper

der linke Fuss

Das ist eine Uhr.
Es ist eine Taschenuhr.

Das ist eine andere Uhr.
Es ist eine Armbanduhr.

Ist das auch eine
Armbanduhr? Nein, das
ist keine Armbanduhr.
Das ist eine Kuckucksuhr.

Ist das eine Kuckucksuhr
oder eine Taschenuhr?
Das ist keine Kuckucksuhr
und keine Taschenuhr,
das ist eine Weckuhr
(ein Wecker).

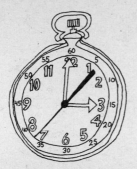

Sechzig (60) Sekunden sind eine Minute. Eine Minute hat 60 Sekunden.

Sechzig (60) Minuten sind eine Stunde. Eine Stunde hat 60 Minuten.

10—zehn
20—zwanzig
30—dreissig
40—vierzig
50—fünfzig
60—sechzig
70—siebzig
80—achtzig
90—neunzig
100—hundert

Ein Tag hat vierundzwanzig (24) Stunden.

1—eins
2—zwei
3—drei
4—vier
5—fünf
6—sechs
7—sieben
8—acht
9—neun
10—zehn
11—elf
12—zwölf
13—dreizehn
14—vierzehn
15—fünfzehn
16—sechzehn
17—siebzehn
18—achtzehn
19—neunzehn
20—zwanzig
21—einundzwanzig
22—zweiundzwanzig
23—dreiundzwanzig
24—vierundzwanzig

Eine Woche hat sieben (7) Tage.
Sieben Tage sind eine Woche.

Montag

Dienstag

Mittwoch

Donnerstag

Freitag

Samstag
(Sonnabend)

Sonntag

Zweiundfünfzig (52) Wochen
sind ein Jahr. Ein Jahr
hat zwölf (12) Monate.

Jeder Monat hat dreissig
(30) oder einunddreissig
(31) Tage. Februar hat nur
achtundzwanzig (28) oder
neunundzwanzig (29) Tage.

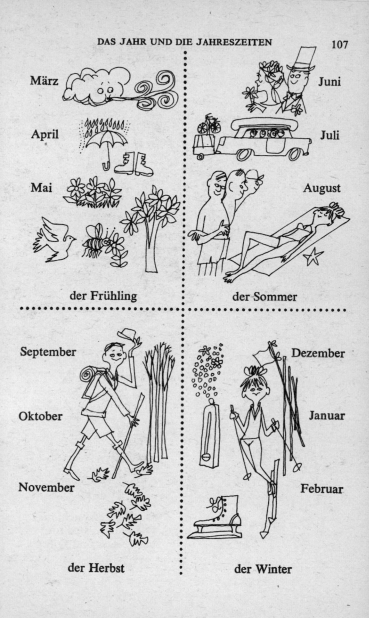

März

Juni

April

Juli

Mai

August

der Frühling

der Sommer

September

Dezember

Oktober

Januar

November

Februar

der Herbst

der Winter

Das Wetter im Frühling
ist schön.
Es ist warm.

Die Luft ist frisch.

Das Gras wächst.
Das Gras ist grün.

Die Blumen wachsen.
Die Blumen sind rot,
blau, weiss und gelb.

Im Sommer ist das Wetter
auch schön.
Es ist heiss.

Wir gehen schwimmen.

Die Blätter wachsen auf
den Bäumen.
Die Bäume sind grün.

Der Tag ist lang.
Die Nacht ist kurz.

Im Herbst ist das Wetter
nicht schön.
Es ist kalt und nass.
Es regnet.

Es ist windig.
Der Wind bläst.

Die Blätter werden rot,
gelb und braun.

Die Blätter fallen
von den Bäumen.

Im Winter ist es kalt.
Es schneit.

Eis und Schnee sind auf
den Strassen.
Alles ist weiss.

Die Bäume haben keine
Blätter. Die Felder haben
keine Blumen.

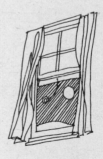

Die Tage sind kurz.
Die Nächte sind lang.

Wieviel Uhr ist es?
Es ist 6 (sechs) Uhr.
Es ist Morgen.
Die Sonne geht auf.

Wieviel Uhr ist es?
Es ist 10 (zehn) Uhr.
Es ist Vormittag. Der
Vormittag ist zwischen
Morgen und Mittag.
Die Sonne scheint.

Wieviel Uhr ist es?
Es ist 12 (zwölf) Uhr.
Es ist Mittag. Scheint die
Sonne? Nein, die Sonne
scheint nicht. Die Sonne
ist hinter den Wolken.

Wieviel Uhr ist es?
Es ist 3 (drei) Uhr.
Es ist Nachmittag. Der
Nachmittag ist zwischen
Mittag und Abend.
Es regnet.

Wieviel Uhr ist es?
Es ist 7 (sieben) Uhr.
Es ist Abend.
Die Sonne geht unter.

Wieviel Uhr ist es?
Es ist 11 (elf) Uhr.
Es ist Nacht.
Der Mond scheint.

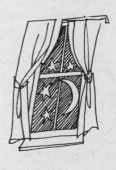

Wieviel Uhr ist es?
Es ist 12 Uhr.
Es ist Mitternacht.
Wir schlafen.

Scheint die Sonne? Nein,
die Sonne scheint nicht.
Der Mond scheint und
die Sterne scheinen.

WIEVIEL UHR IST ES?
(*Wie spät ist es?*)

ein Viertel

halb

drei Viertel

eine Stunde

Es ist zwei **Uhr**.

Es ist zwei Uhr zehn.
Es ist zehn Minuten
nach zwei.

Es ist zwei Uhr fünfzehn
(15). Es ist 15 Minuten
nach zwei. Es ist ein
Viertel nach zwei.
Es ist Viertel drei.

Es ist zwei Uhr dreissig
(30). Es ist 30 Minuten
nach zwei. Es ist
halb drei.

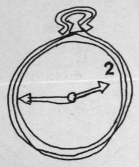

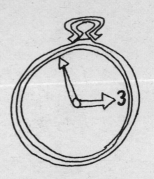

Es ist zwei Uhr
fünfundvierzig (45).
Es ist fünfzehn Minuten
vor drei. Es ist ein
Viertel vor drei. Es ist
drei Viertel drei.

Es ist zwei Uhr
fünfundfünfzig (55).
Es ist fünf Minuten
vor drei.

Es ist drei Uhr.

Es ist fünfzehn Uhr.
(15:00). Es ist drei
Uhr nachmittags.

Wieviel Uhr ist es?
Es ist sieben Uhr (7:00).
Es ist Morgen.
Der Tag beginnt.

Der Wecker läutet.

Herr und Frau Schmidt
stehen auf.
"Guten Morgen, Anna!"
"Guten Morgen, Willy!"

"Kinder!" ruft Frau
Schmidt. "Steht auf!" "Wir
müssen alle aufstehen!"

118

Karl und Otto stehen
langsam auf. Karl gähnt.
Er ist noch müde.

Gretchen will nicht
aufstehen. Sie will länger
schlafen. "Gretchen!" ruft
die Mutter. "Aufstehen!
Es ist spät!"

Karl und Otto ziehen
sich an.

Gretchen zieht sich
auch an.

das Unterhemd

 die Hosen

die Unterhose

die Jacke
der Rock

die Socken

der Anzug

das Hemd

 die Weste

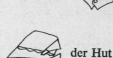

der Schlips

der Hut

der Gürtel

die Mütze
die Kappe

der Büstenhalter

das Kostüm

der Unterrock

die Schuhe

die Bluse

die Handschuhe

die Strümpfe

das Taschentuch

der Rock

die Handtasche

das Kleid

der Mantel

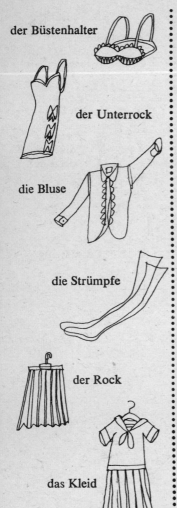
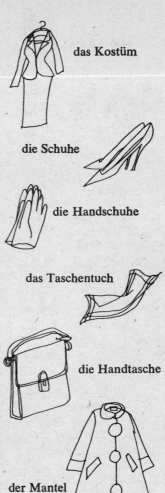

Herr Schmidt ist im
Badezimmer. Er wäscht sich.
Er wäscht sich mit Seife
und mit einem
Waschlappen. Er wäscht
sich mit warmem Wasser.

Er putzt sich die Zähne.
Er hat eine Zahnbürste
und Zahnpaste. Er putzt
sich die Zähne mit
kaltem Wasser.

Er rasiert sich. Er hat
Rasierseife im Gesicht
und einen Rasierapparat
in der Hand. Er rasiert
sich mit heissem Wasser.

Er trocknet seine Hände
und sein Gesicht mit
einem Handtuch.

Herr Schmidt ist noch im Badezimmer. Es ist spät. Karl und Otto warten vor der Tür.

Gretchen ist in ihrem Zimmer. Sie sitzt vor ihrem Spiegel.

Sie kämmt und bürstet ihr Haar.

Sie trägt °Lippenstift auf.

Frau Schmidt ist in der
Küche. Sie kocht Frühstück
für ihre Familie.

Die Kinder trinken Milch.
Sie trinken ein Glas
Milch. Fritz und Mimi
trinken auch Milch.

Die Eltern trinken
Kaffee. Sie trinken eine
Tasse Kaffee.

Hier ist die Milchflasche
und die Kaffeekanne.

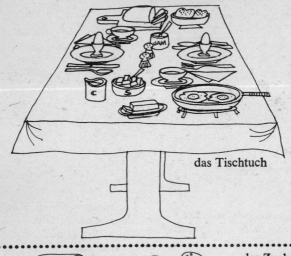

das Tischtuch

der Zucker

das Brot

das Salz    der Pfeffer

die Serviette

der Teller

die Gabel

das Messer

der Löffel

das Brötchen

die Spiegeleier

die Sahne

die Tasse

die Marmelade

die Untertasse

ein
weichgekochtes
Ei

die Bratpfanne

der Eierbecher

die Butter

Der Vater hört Radio.
Er hört die Nachrichten.
Dann geht er ins Geschäft.
"Auf Wiedersehen!"

Karl und Otto gehen in
die Schule.
"Auf Wiedersehen!"

Gretchen geht arbeiten.
"Auf Wiedersehen!"

Die Mutter wäscht
das Geschirr.

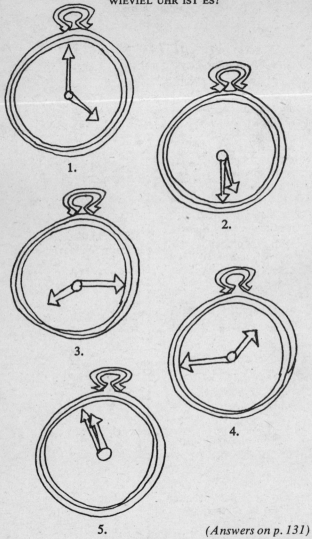

1.

2.

3.

4.

5.

(Answers on p. 131)

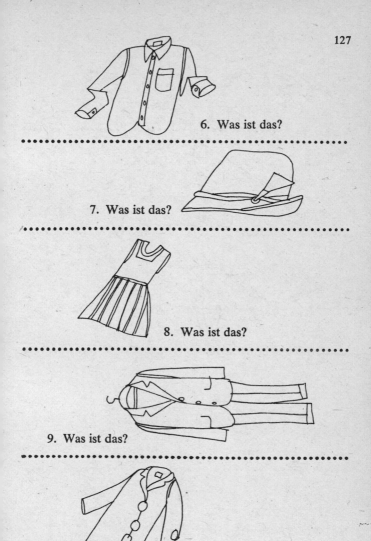

6. Was ist das?

7. Was ist das?

8. Was ist das?

9. Was ist das?

10. Was ist das?

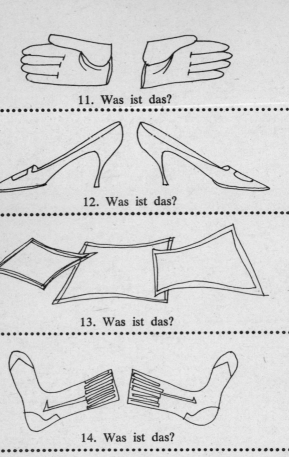

11. Was ist das?

12. Was ist das?

13. Was ist das?

14. Was ist das?

15. Was ist das?

**16. Was tut der Wecker?**

**17. Was tut Karl?**

**18. Was tut Herr Schmidt?**

**19. Was tut Gretchen?**

20. Wo ist die Familie?

21. Was tut Frau Schmidt?

22. Was tut Herr Schmidt?

23. Was tun Fritz und Mimi?

## ANTWORTEN

1. Es ist vier Uhr.
2. Es ist halb sechs.
3. Es ist Viertel neun.
4. Es ist drei Viertel zwei.
5. Es ist zehn Minuten vor zwölf.
6. Das ist ein Hemd.
7. Das ist ein Hut.
8. Das ist ein Kleid.
9. Das ist ein Anzug.
10. Das ist ein Mantel.
11. Das sind Handschuhe (zwei Handschuhe).
12. Das sind Schuhe (ein Paar Schuhe).
13. Das sind Taschentücher (drei Taschentücher)
14. Das sind Socken.
15. Das sind Strümpfe.
16. Der Wecker läutet. Er läutet.
17. Er zieht sich an.
18. Er wäscht sich.
19. Sie kämmt ihr Haar.
20. Die Familie ist in der Küche.
21. Sie kocht Frühstück.
22. Er trinkt eine Tasse Kaffee.
23. Sie trinken Milch.

Karl und Otto gehen in die
Schule. Wohin gehen sie?
Sie gehen in die Schule.

Otto geht mit Karl.
Er geht mit ihm.

Er geht mit seinem Bruder.
Wo sind Karl und Otto?
Sie sind auf der Strasse.

Hier kommt die
Strassenbahn. Sie kommt
die Strasse entlang.

Otto steigt ein.
Karl steigt ein.
Sie steigen ein.

Die Strassenbahn fährt weg.

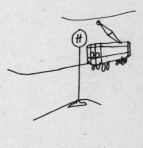

Wo sind Karl und Otto
jetzt? Sie sind jetzt in
der Strassenbahn.

Der Schaffner kommt.
"Fahrkarten, bitte!"

Karl und Otto kaufen
Fahrkarten. Karl kauft
eine Fahrkarte für sich
und eine Fahrkarte für
seinen Bruder.

Karl gibt dem Schaffner
Geld. Er gibt ihm Geld.
Er gibt es ihm.

Der Schaffner nimmt
das Geld. Er nimmt es.

Der Schaffner gibt Karl
zwei Fahrkarten. Er gibt
ihm zwei Fahrkarten.
Er gibt sie ihm.

Karl nimmt die
Fahrkarten. Er nimmt sie.

Er gibt seinem Bruder
eine Fahrkarte. Er gibt
sie seinem Bruder.
Er gibt sie ihm.

Die andere Fahrkarte ist
für ihn selbst.

"Schillerplatz!" ruft
der Schaffner.

Die Strassenbahn hält.

Karl und Otto steigen aus.

Hier ist ihre Schule.

Wo sind Karl und Otto?
Sie sind in der Schule.

Karl ist im Klassenzimmer.

Das Klassenzimmer hat
ein Pult und einen Stuhl
für den Lehrer

und viele Pulte und
Stühle für die Schüler.

Das Klassenzimmer hat
eine Wandtafel.
Die Tafel ist schwarz.

An der anderen Wand ist
eine Landkarte.
Die Landkarte zeigt Europa.
Die Landkarte ist bunt.

Das Klassenzimmer hat eine
Tür und drei Fenster.

Ein Fenster ist offen
(auf) und die zwei
anderen Fenster sind zu.

Ich mache das Fenster auf.

Ich mache das Fenster zu.

**Wann beginnt die Schule?**
**Sie beginnt um neun Uhr.**

Jetzt ist es neun Uhr.
Der Lehrer kommt.
Die Stunde beginnt.

Der Lehrer kommt in das
Klassenzimmer.
"Guten Morgen, Kinder!"

Die Schüler stehen auf.
In Deutschland stehen
die Kinder immer auf,
wenn der Lehrer kommt.

"Guten Morgen,
Herr Lehrer!"

Die Schüler setzen sich.

Jeder Schüler hat
ein Pult. Hier ist
Karls Pult.

In diesem Pult hat
er seine Bücher.

Er hat auch ein Heft, eine
Feder und einen Bleistift.

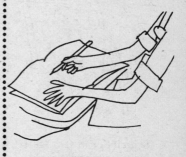

Er schreibt in sein Heft.
Er schreibt mit der Feder.

Der Lehrer schreibt auch.
Schreibt er auch mit
einer Feder oder mit
einem Bleistift?
Nein, er schreibt nicht
mit der Feder oder mit
dem Bleistift, er schreibt
mit Kreide.

Er hat ein Stück
Kreide in der Hand.

Schreibt er in sein Heft?
Nein, er schreibt nicht
in sein Heft.
Er schreibt an die Tafel.

Er schreibt mit Kreide
an die Tafel.

Was schreibt der Lehrer?
Er schreibt Wörter und
Sätze. Er schreibt
englische Wörter.

Was lernen die Schüler?
Sie lernen Englisch.
Sie sprechen Deutsch und
sie lernen Englisch.

Der Lehrer fragt:
"Ist Englisch schwer?"

Karl antwortet: "Englisch
ist schwer für mich.
Aber es ist nicht
schwer für Sie."

"Ist Englisch schwerer
als Deutsch?"
fragt der Lehrer.

"Für einen Deutschen ist
Englisch schwerer als
Deutsch," antwortet Karl.

Aber für einen Engländer
ist Englisch leicht.

Für einen Engländer ist
Englisch leichter
als Deutsch.

Der Lehrer sagt:
"Ich spreche Englisch.
Ich kann gut
Englisch sprechen."

Er fragt: "Sprechen Sie
auch Englisch?
Können Sie auch gut
Englisch sprechen?"

Die Schüler antworten:
"Wir sprechen ein wenig
Englisch. Aber wir
können nicht gut sprechen."

Der Lehrer spricht gut.
Die Schüler sprechen
nicht so gut. Der Lehrer
spricht besser als die Schüler.

Der Lehrer spricht schnell.

Ein Schüler sagt:
"Bitte, Herr Lehrer,
sprechen Sie nicht
so schnell! Ich kann
Sie nicht verstehen."

"Bitte, wiederholen Sie!
Bitte, sprechen Sie
langsam. Wenn Sie
langsamer sprechen, kann
ich Sie besser verstehen."

Der Lehrer spricht jetzt
langsam. Er wiederholt
alles. Er sagt es
noch einmal.

Der Lehrer fragt:
"Können Sie alles
verstehen? Haben Sie
eine Frage?"

Karl kann nicht alles
verstehen. Er hat eine
Frage. Er hebt die Hand.

"Herr Lehrer, ich habe
eine Frage. Ich kann das
nicht verstehen. Können
Sie es erklären, bitte?"

Der Lehrer erklärt alles.
Er sagt es noch einmal.
Jetzt können die
Schüler verstehen.

Der Lehrer spricht.
Er wiederholt alles.
Er spricht laut.

Karl spricht auch.
Er spricht mit einem
anderen Jungen. Aber er
spricht nicht laut.
Er spricht leise.

Er hat Glück. Der Lehrer
hört ihn nicht.
Der Lehrer spricht weiter.

Die Glocke läutet.
Die Stunde ist zu Ende.
Der Lehrer geht aus
der Klasse.

Es ist Mittagspause.
Karl und Otto essen
in der Schule.

Karl hat ein Butterbrot
mit Leberwurst. Er isst es.
Es schmeckt gut.

Otto hat ein Käsebrot.
Er isst es.
Es schmeckt auch gut.
Es ist sehr gut.

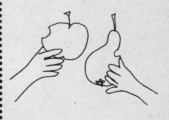

Karl isst auch einen Apfel
und Otto isst eine Birne.
Sie essen ihr Mittagessen
in der Schule.

Jetzt ist es drei Uhr.
Die Glocke läutet wieder.

Die Schule ist jetzt aus.
Karl und Otto kommen aus
der Schule.

Sie gehen nach Hause.

Von wo kommen sie? Sie
kommen aus der Schule.
Wo sind sie? Sie sind
auf der Strasse.
Wohin gehen sie?
Sie gehen nach Hause.

Es ist Morgen. Gretchen
geht aus dem Haus.

Geht sie auch in die
Schule? Nein, sie geht
nicht in die Schule.
Sie geht arbeiten.

Wie kommt sie zur Arbeit?
Sie fährt mit dem Autobus.

Der Autobus bringt
sie zur Arbeit.

Gretchen arbeitet in
einem Warenhaus.

Ein Warenhaus ist ein
grosses Geschäft.
Es hat viele Abteilungen.

Diese Abteilung ist
im Erdgeschoss.
Diese Abteilung
verkauft Kleider.

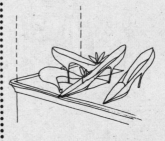

Hier kann man
Schuhe kaufen.

Wir sind im ersten Stock.
Hier ist die Abteilung
für Papier und Schreibwaren.

Verzeihen Sie bitte,
können Sie mir sagen,
wo ich Toiletteartikel
finden kann?
Im zweiten Stock.

Ich nehme den Aufzug zum
dritten Stock.
Hier sind Haushaltartikel
und Geschirr.

Und hier sind Nähzeug
und Kurzwaren.

Hier ist die Rolltreppe
zum vierten Stock.
Diese Abteilung hat
Bettwäsche und
Tischwäsche.

Hier kann man
Stoffe kaufen.

Diese Treppe führt
zum Souterrain.
Diese Abteilung verkauft
Werkzeuge und Eisenwaren.

Und hier ist eine
Abteilung für Kinder:
Spielzeug.

Gretchen arbeitet hier.
Sie verkauft Spiele.

Sie verkauft viele
schöne Puppen.

Sie verkauft Bälle
und Pistolen

und elektrische Eisenbahnen.

Gretchen verkauft
viele Spielsachen.

Ein Kunde kommt.

"Fräulein, können Sie
mir helfen?"

"Natürlich, sehr gern.
Womit kann ich dienen?"

"Ich möchte ein Geschenk
für meinen kleinen
Jungen kaufen."

"Wie alt ist der Junge?"
"Er ist acht Jahre alt."

"Können Sie mir
etwas zeigen?"

Gretchen bringt
eine Schachtel.

"Hier ist ein Feuerwehrwagen.
Er ist sehr schön und nicht teuer."

"Wieviel kostet das?"

"Es kostet 12 (zwölf) Mark."

"Das ist zu viel. Haben Sie etwas anderes?
Haben Sie etwas billigeres?"

Gretchen bringt
viele Schachteln.

Sie muss dem Mann viele
Dinge zeigen.

Endlich kauft er einen Lastwagen.

Der Lastwagen kostet nur zwei Mark siebzig.
Das ist billig.

Gretchen packt die
Schachtel ein. Sie gibt
dem Mann das Paket.

Der Mann gibt ihr
einen Zehnmarkschein.

Gretchen gibt ihm
Kleingeld. Er bekommt sieben Mark
dreissig Kleingeld.

Ein Fünfmarkschein, ein
Markstück, zwei
Fünfzigpfennigstücke und
drei Zehnpfennigstücke.

"Danke sehr!
Auf Wiedersehen."

Der Mann nimmt das Paket
und das Kleingeld.
Er geht weg.

Gretchen muss
schwer arbeiten.

Sie ist den ganzen Tag auf
den Füssen. Sie ist müde.

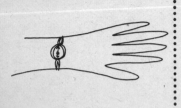

Es ist sechs Uhr. Gretchens
Arbeitstag ist zu Ende.

Sie schliesst die Kasse.

Sie zieht ihren Mantel
an. Sie geht nach Hause.

Wie kommt sie nach Hause?
Geht sie zu Fuss? Nein,
sie nimmt den Autobus.

1. Wohin gehen Karl und Otto?

2. Wie fahren sie?

3. Was kaufen sie?

4. Wann beginnt die Schule?

164

5. Was tun die Schüler, wenn der Lehrer kommt?

6. Schreibt der Lehrer mit einer Feder?

7. Schreibt Karl an die Tafel?

8. Was lernen die Schüler?

9. Was hat Otto zum
Mittagessen?

10. Wann ist die Schule aus?

11. Geht Gretchen auch
in die Schule?

12. Wo arbeitet sie?

13. Wo kann man
Schreibwaren kaufen?

14. Welche Abteilung
ist im Erdgeschoss?

15. Wo arbeitet Gretchen?

16. Was möchte der
Kunde kaufen?

17. Wieviel kostet der
Feuerwehrwagen?

18. Was muss Gretchen tun?

19. Wieviel Kleingeld
bekommt der Mann?

20. Wie kommt Gretchen
am Abend nach Hause?

### ANTWORTEN

1. Sie gehen in die Schule.
2. Sie fahren mit der Strassenbahn.
3. Sie kaufen Fahrkarten.
4. Die Schule beginnt um neun Uhr.
5. Die Schüler stehen auf, wenn der Lehrer kommt.
6. Nein, er schreibt mit Kreide.
7. Nein, er schreibt nicht an die Tafel,
   er schreibt in sein Heft.
8. Sie lernen Englisch.
9. Er hat ein Käsebrot und eine Birne.
10. Die Schule ist um drei Uhr aus.
11. Nein, sie geht nicht in die Schule,
    sie geht arbeiten.
12. Sie arbeitet in einem Warenhaus.
13. Man kann Schreibwaren im ersten Stock kaufen.
14. Die Abteilung für Kleider ist im Erdgeschoss.
15. Sie arbeitet in der Spielzeugabteilung.
16. Er möchte ein Geschenk für seinen
    kleinen Jungen kaufen.
17. Er kostet zwölf Mark.
18. Sie muss dem Mann viele Dinge zeigen.
19. Er bekommt sieben Mark dreissig Kleingeld.
20. Sie nimmt den Autobus.

Herr Schmidt geht
aus dem Haus.

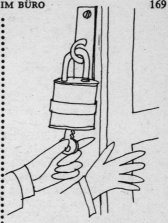

Er geht zur Garage.
Er öffnet die Tür.

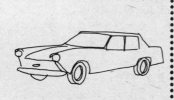

Hier ist Herrn Schmidts
Auto. Er hat einen
grossen Wagen.

Er öffnet die Tür.
Er steigt ein.

# DAS AUTO

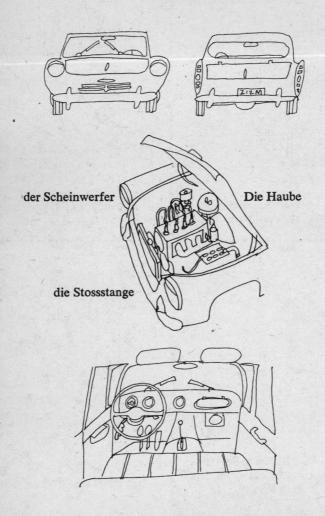

der Scheinwerfer

Die Haube

die Stossstange

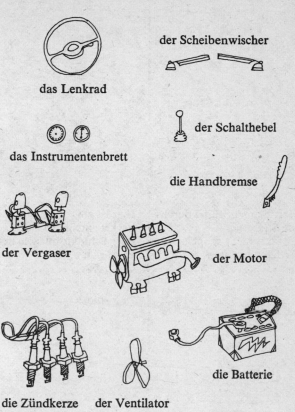

das Lenkrad

der Scheibenwischer

das Instrumentenbrett

der Schalthebel

die Handbremse

der Vergaser

der Motor

die Zündkerze     der Ventilator

die Batterie

die (Fuss)bremse

die Kupplung  der Gashebel

der Kühler

Herr Schmidt fährt durch
die Strassen.
Er fährt nicht schnell.
Er fährt langsam.

Hier ist ein
Verkehrslicht. Es ist rot.
Herr Schmidt muss halten.
Er wartet.

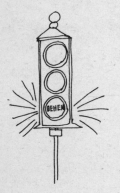

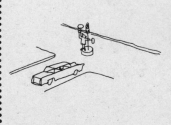

Das Licht wird gelb.
Herr Schmidt wartet noch.
Jetzt ist es grün.
Herr Schmidt fährt weiter.

Hier ist eine Kreuzung.
Zwei Strassen kommen
zusammen.
Hier steht ein Polizist.
Herr Schmidt wartet wieder.

Herr Schmidt kommt zu
einer Tankstelle.
Er hält an.

Der Tankwart kommt.
"Womit kann ich
Ihnen dienen?"

"Füllen Sie den Wagen mit
Benzin, bitte.
Und bitte, kontrollieren
Sie auch das Öl und
das Wasser im Kühler."

Der Tankwart tut alles.
"Sie haben genug Öl und
Sie brauchen auch
kein Wasser."

Der Tankwart wäscht die
Windschutzscheibe.

"Zehn Liter Benzin zu
2 M 50 macht 25 Mark."

Herr Schmidt zahlt ihm.
"Vielen Dank!
Kommen Sie bald wieder!"

Herr Schmidt fährt weg.

In dieser Strasse ist
Herrn Schmidts Büro.

Aber in dieser Strasse
kann man nicht parken.
Parken ist hier verboten.

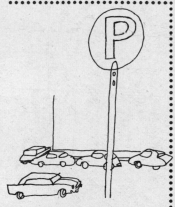

In dieser Strasse ist
Parken erlaubt.
Aber Herr Schmidt kann
keinen Parkplatz finden.

Er muss den Wagen zu
einem öffentlichen
Parkplatz bringen.

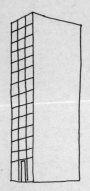

Hier ist ein grosses
Geschäftshaus. Herrn Schmidts Büro
ist in diesem Haus.

Sein Büro ist im 15. Stock.
Er muss den Aufzug nehmen.

"Guten Morgen,
Herr Schmidt,"
sagt der Liftjunge.

"Guten Morgen,
Herr Schmidt!" "Guten Morgen,
Fräulein Ilse!" Fräulein Ilse ist Herrn
Schmidts Sekretärin.

Fräulein Ilse ist sehr
hübsch. Sie ist ein
hübsches Mädchen.

Sie hat eine gute Figur.
Sie hat ein
hübsches Gesicht.

Herr Schmidt hat hübsche
Sekretärinnen gern.

"Wie geht's heute?"
"Danke, gut. Und wie
geht es Ihnen?"
"Danke, es geht mir
auch gut."

"Habe ich heute Post?"
"Ja, natürlich. Sie
liegt schon
auf Ihrem Schreibtisch."

Auf dem Schreibtisch
liegen viele Briefe.
Hier ist auch eine
Photographie von Herrn
Schmidts Familie.

Herr Schmidt nimmt einen
Brief von seinem
Schreibtisch. Er öffnet
den Brief. Er liest ihn.

Er diktiert eine Antwort.

Fräulein Ilse schreibt
den Brief. Sie tippt ihn auf
ihrer Schreibmaschine.

Dann tippt sie den
Briefumschlag mit
der Adresse.

Sie bringt Herrn
Schmidt den Brief.

Er unterschreibt ihn.

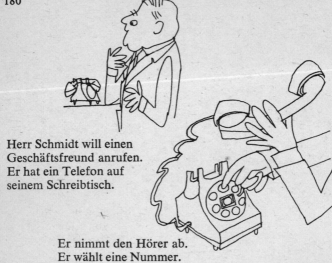

Herr Schmidt will einen
Geschäftsfreund anrufen.
Er hat ein Telefon auf
seinem Schreibtisch.

Er nimmt den Hörer ab.
Er wählt eine Nummer.

"Hallo! Ist das
Steinberg & Co.?"
"Nein, Sie sind falsch
verbunden." "Entschuldigen
Sie, bitte."

Herr Schmidt hängt ab.
Er ist zornig.

Herr Schmidt nimmt
das Telefonbuch.

Er sucht die Nummer
seines Freundes.

Er ruft wieder an.
Antwortet sein
Freund diesmal?

Nein, sein Freund
antwortet nicht.
Die Nummer ist besetzt.

Später versucht Herr
Schmidt es noch einmal.

Er hört ein Signal.
Das Telefon läutet im
Büro seines Freundes.
Sein Freund ist da.

Er antwortet
"Hallo, hier Steinberg."

Herr Schmidt und
Herr Steinberg
sprechen miteinander.

Die Sekretärin klopft
an die Tür. "Herein!"

"Ein Herr Tauber möchte
Sie sprechen.
Er wartet auf Sie."

"Lassen Sie ihn
hereinkommen!"

"Bitte, setzen Sie sich!"
Herr Tauber setzt sich.
Er spricht lange mit
Herrn Schmidt.

Herr Schmidt hat
viele Besucher.

Er macht viele
Telefonanrufe.

Er diktiert
viele Briefe.

Fräulein Ilse hat
viel zu tun.

"Fräulein Ilse, diese
Briefe sind sehr wichtig.
Sie müssen sie zur Post
bringen. Wissen Sie,
wo das Postamt ist?"

"Nein, Herr Schmidt,
das weiss ich nicht.
Können
Sie mir sagen, wie
ich zum Postamt komme?"

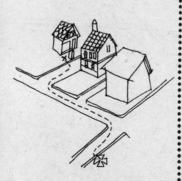

"Das Postamt ist nicht
weit. Geradeaus, die
erste Strasse links,
und dann die zweite
Strasse rechts."

Hier ist das Postamt.
Es ist gegenüber
vom Rathaus.

Auf dem Postamt sind
viele Leute.
Sie stehen Schlange.

Fräulein Ilse geht zum
Schalter. Sie will
Briefmarken kaufen.

Der Postbeamte verkauft
Briefmarken: gewöhnliche
Briefmarken und
Luftpostmarken.

Fräulein Ilse wirft
die Briefe
in den Briefkasten.

## PAKETE

Hier ist der Schalter
für Pakete.

## TELEGRAMME

An diesem Schalter kann
man Telegramme aufgeben.

## EINGESCHRIEBENEBRIEFE

Hier ist ein Schalter für
eingeschriebene Briefe.
Wichtige Briefe werden
eingeschrieben.

## POSTANWEISUNGEN

Und hier bekommt man
Postanweisungen.
Mit einer Postanweisung
schickt man Geld.

Karl und Otto sind
in der Schule.

Gretchen arbeitet
im Geschäft.

Herr Schmidt ist im Büro.

Frau Schmidt bleibt
zu Hause.
Sie hat viel zu tun.

Sie wäscht das
Frühstücksgeschirr.

Sie stellt das
Geschirr weg.

Sie macht die Betten.

Sie staubt die Möbel ab.

Sie macht den
Fussboden rein.

Sie reinigt den Teppich
mit dem Staubsauger.

Sie wäscht die Kleider
in der Waschmaschine.

Sie bügelt (plättet) die
Kleider auf dem Bügelbrett
mit dem Bügeleisen.

Frau Schmidt ist müde.

Sie setzt sich nieder.
Sie ruht sich aus.

Sie sieht ein
Fernsehprogramm.

Sie schreibt einen Brief.

Sie ruft eine
Freundin an.

Sie spricht am Telefon.

Sie spricht lange.

Endlich ist das
Gespräch zu Ende.

Frau Schmidt muss
einkaufen gehen.

Sie nimmt ein
Stück Papier. Sie macht
sich eine Liste.

Sie schreibt viele
Dinge auf.

Sie nimmt ihre
Einkaufstasche.

Zuerst geht Frau Schmidt
zu einem Bäcker.
Hier kauft sie Brot
und Semmeln.

Der Bäcker verkauft
auch Torten und Kuchen.

Dann geht sie zum
Fleischer.
Der Fleischer hat
Schweinefleisch,
Rindfleisch, Kalbfleisch,
Hammelfleisch und
Geflügel.

Er hat Schinken, Speck,
Würste und
kalten Aufschnitt.

Hier ist ein
Gemüsehändler.
Hier bekommt man frisches
Obst und Gemüse:

Äpfel und Birnen

Kirschen und Bananen

Trauben und Nüsse

Kartoffeln und Tomaten

Karotten und Erbsen

Mais und Salat

Bohnen, Kohl und viele
andere gute Dinge.

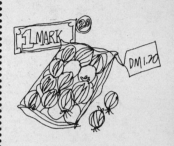

Frau Schmidt braucht
drei Pfund Zwiebeln.

Sie kosten
1 M 20 das Pfund.

"Sind die Pilze frisch?"
fragt sie.
"Aber natürlich," sagt
die Gemüsefrau.
"Sie sind ganz frisch."

"Gut, dann geben Sie mir
ein Pfund."
"Sonst noch etwas?"
"Nein, das ist genug
für heute.
Das ist alles."

Nun geht Frau Schmidt
zu einem Milchladen.

Sie kauft zwei
Liter Milch,

ein halbes Pfund
Butter und ein
viertel Pfund Käse

und ein Dutzend Eier.

Endlich geht Frau Schmidt
zu einem
Kolonialwarenhändler.

Hier kauft man
Kaffee und Tee

Zucker und Salz

Essig und Öl
und viele Gewürze.

Frau Schmidt kauft
viele Dinge.

Alles kostet viel Geld.

Ihre Einkaufstasche
ist voll und schwer.

Sie bringt alles
nach Hause.

*(Antworten auf Seite 206)*

1. Wie kommt Herr Schmidt
von seinem Haus
zu seinem Büro?

2. Was für ein
Auto hat er?

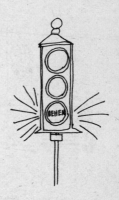

3. Warum muss
Herr Schmidt halten?

4. Wann fährt er weiter?

5. Was tut er an der Tankstelle?

6. Warum kann er in dieser Strasse nicht parken?

7. Wo lässt Herr Schmidt seinen Wagen?

8. Wie sieht Fräulein Ilse aus?

9. Wer ist
Herr Steinberg?

10. Wohin geht die
Sekretärin nach
der Arbeit?

11. Was macht Frau Schmidt
nach dem Frühstück?

12. Was tut sie mit
den Kleidern?

13. Wen ruft
Frau Schmidt an?

14. Wohin muss sie gehen?

15. Zu wem geht
sie zuerst?

16. Was verkauft
ein Fleischer?

17. Was kann man in einem
Gemüseladen kaufen?

18. Wieviel kosten
die Zwiebeln?

19. Wo bekommt man
Butter und Käse?

20. Was macht Frau Schmidt
mit all den Dingen,
die sie gekauft hat?

### ANTWORTEN

1. Er fährt mit dem Auto.
2. Er hat einen grossen Wagen.
3. Das Licht ist rot.
4. Er fährt weiter, wenn das Licht grün ist.
5. Er kauft Benzin. Er braucht Benzin.
   Er will tanken.
6. Parken ist hier verboten.
   Parken ist nicht erlaubt.
7. Er lässt den Wagen in einem öffentlichen Parkplatz.
8. Sie ist hübsch.
9. Er ist ein Geschäftsfreund von Herrn Schmidt.
10. Sie geht zum Postamt.
11. Sie wäscht das Geschirr.
12. Sie wäscht und bügelt die Kleider.
13. Sie ruft eine Freundin an.
14. Sie muss einkaufen gehen.
15. Sie geht zum Bäcker.
16. Er verkauft Fleisch und Wurst.
17. Man kann Obst und Gemüse kaufen.
18. Sie kosten eine Mark zwanzig das Pfund.
19. Man bekommt Butter und Käse in
    einem Milchladen.
20. Sie tut sie in die Einkaufstasche und bringt
    alles nach Hause.

Karl und Otto kommen
von der Schule.

Sie kommen nach Hause.

Sie sind hungrig
und durstig.

Sie trinken ein Glas
Milch und essen
ein Stück Kuchen.

"Jetzt ist es Zeit
für die Schulaufgaben,"
sagt die Mutter.

"Noch nicht!
Es ist noch nicht spät.
Wir haben noch Zeit.

Wir machen unsere
Aufgaben später.
Wir wollen mit unseren
Freunden spielen."

"Gut, aber nur bis
fünf Uhr."

Die zwei Jungen laufen
aus dem Haus.

Sie laufen zu ihrem
Freund.
"Hans, komm mit uns!
Wir gehen Ball spielen."

Die Jungen laufen
zum Spielplatz.

Sie spielen Fussball.

Es ist spät.
Es wird dunkel.

Die Jungen kommen wieder
nach Hause. Jetzt müssen
sie ihre Aufgaben machen.

Sie gehen auf ihr Zimmer,
zünden das Licht an, und
nehmen ihre Schulbücher.

Sie studieren fleissig.

Gretchen kommt auch
nach Hause.

Sie geht in ihr Zimmer.
Sie ist müde.

Sie liest eine
Zeitschrift.

Sie spielt Schallplatten
auf ihrem Grammophon.

Nun kommt Herr Schmidt
auch nach Hause.
Er bringt den Wagen
in die Garage.

Er schliesst die
Tür zur Garage ab.

Er setzt sich in einen
Sessel im Wohnzimmer.

Er liest die Zeitung.

Frau Schmidt ist in der Küche.
Sie kocht das Abendessen.

Sie deckt den Tisch.
Gretchen hilft ihr.

Jetzt sitzt die Familie
um den Tisch.
Sie essen das Abendessen.

Nach dem Abendessen
geht Gretchen
wieder in ihr Zimmer.
Sie zieht sich um.

Sie schminkt sich.
Sie macht sich schön.
Sie hat eine Verabredung.

Ihr Freund kommt
sie abholen.

Gretchen ist noch
nicht fertig.
Er muss auf sie warten.

"Was sollen wir heute
Abend tun?" "Ich möchte
ins Kino gehen. Man
spielt einen guten Film."

Er kauft die Kinokarten.
Sie gehen ins Kino.

Nach dem Kino gehen
sie in ein Kaffeehaus.

Gretchen kommt spät
nach Hause. "Gute Nacht!"

Herr und Frau Schmidt
haben Besuch.

Ihre Freunde,
die Müllers, kommen.

Herr Müller legt Hut und Mantel ab.
Frau Müller hat eine Pelzjacke.

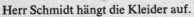

Herr Schmidt hängt die Kleider auf.

Die Schmidts und
die Müllers sitzen
im Wohnzimmer.

Sie spielen Karten.
Sie rauchen.

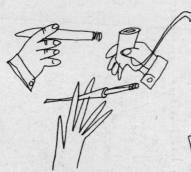

Frau Schmidt raucht eine
Zigarette, Herr Schmidt
eine Zigarre und
Herr Müller raucht
eine Pfeife.
Frau Müller raucht nicht.

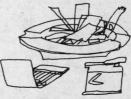

Hier sind Streichhölzer
und ein Feuerzeug.
Der Aschenbecher ist voll.

Karl und Otto müssen
mehr studieren.

Morgen haben sie
eine Prüfung.

Endlich sind sie
fertig. Jetzt ist es spät.
Sie ziehen sich aus.

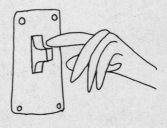

Sie löschen das Licht
aus. Sie gehen zu Bett.
Sie schlafen ein.

Heute ist Sonntag.
Herr Schmidt geht
nicht ins Büro.

Gretchen geht
nicht arbeiten.

Karl und Otto gehen
nicht in die Schule.

Alle können
länger schlafen.

Sie ziehen ihre
guten Kleider an.

Sie gehen in die Kirche.

Nach der Kirche gehen
sie spazieren.
Sie gehen in den Park.

Der Park ist schön.
Hier ist ein kleiner See.

Im Park gibt es Wiesen und Bäume,

Spielplätze für Kinder

und Bänke für alte Leute.

Am Nachmittag
besuchen die Kinder
ihre Grosseltern

oder sie gehen
in ein Museum

oder sie gehen kegeln

oder sie gehen zu
einem Fussballspiel.

Manchmal gehen sie
zu einer Ausstellung

oder in ein Konzert

oder zu einem Vortrag

oder ins Theater.

Am Abend sagt der Vater: "Heute Abend essen wir nicht zu Hause.

Wir gehen aus. Wir gehen in ein Restaurant."

Alle sind sehr froh.

Frau Schmidt ist froh.
Sie braucht nicht zu kochen.

Sie kommen in das
Restaurant. Es heisst
"Zum Goldenen Löwen."

"Einen Tisch für
fünf, bitte!"

Der Kellner führt sie
zu einem Tisch.

Sie setzen sich.

Von diesem Tisch kann
man das ganze
Restaurant sehen.

An einem Ende ist die Bar.
Hier ist der Mixer.

Am anderen Ende spielt
ein kleines Orchester:

Ein Klavier, eine Geige
und eine Ziehharmonika.

Der Kellner bringt
die Speisekarte
und die Weinkarte.
"Möchten Sie etwas
zu trinken?"

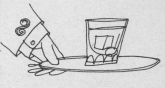

Frau Schmidt bestellt
einen Apéritif.

Gretchen trinkt
ein Glas Wein.

Herr Schmidt bestellt
eine Flasche Bier.

"Beginnen wir mit
der Vorspeise!" sagt Herr
Schmidt. "Ich nehme
eine Leberpastete."

Frau Schmidt sagt:
"Ich möchte
einen Hering."

"Bringen Sie mir ein Glas
Fruchtsaft, bitte!"
sagt Gretchen.

"Und ich nehme lieber
einen Teller Suppe,"
Sagt Karl.
"Ich auch," sagt Otto.

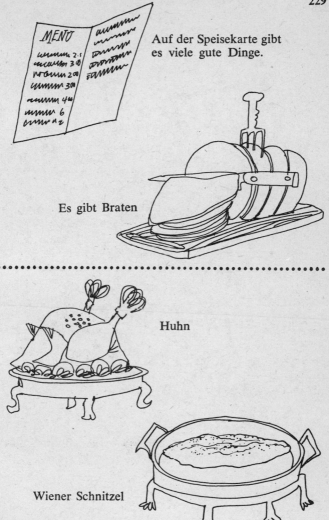

Auf der Speisekarte gibt
es viele gute Dinge.

Es gibt Braten

Huhn

Wiener Schnitzel

Fisch

Schweinskotelett

Bratwurst mit Sauerkraut

oder Sauerbraten mit Knödel.

Der Kellner bringt auch Kartoffeln,

Gemüse,

Salat

und Brot und Butter.

232

Zum Nachtisch gibt
es Kuchen

oder Eis mit Keks.

Herr und Frau Schmidt
trinken Kaffee.

Gretchen trinkt Tee
mit Zitrone. Karl und Otto
trinken Milch.

Das Essen war sehr gut.

"Herr Ober, zahlen!"

Der Kellner bringt
die Rechnung.

Das Essen kostet nicht
zu viel.
Dieses Restaurant ist
nicht sehr teuer.

Herr Schmidt gibt dem
Kellner ein Trinkgeld.
"Danke vielmals!
Kommen Sie bald wieder!"

Sie gehen zur Garderobe
und holen ihre Mäntel.

Jetzt gehen sie langsam
nach Hause.

Es war ein schöner Abend.

Herr Schmidt ist im Bett.

Er fühlt sich nicht wohl.

Er hat Kopfschmerzen.

Er hat Halsschmerzen.

236

Er hustet.

Er niest.

Er hat einen Schnupfen.

Er hat eine Erkältung.

Er ist heiser. Er kann nicht laut sprechen.

Er hat Fieber.

Seine Frau ruft einen Arzt an. Sie lässt den Arzt kommen.

Der Arzt kommt. Er heisst Dr. Kesselmann.

"Guten Tag, Herr Doktor," sagt Frau Schmidt.

"Es freut mich, dass Sie kommen konnten.

• • • • • • • • • • • • • • • • • • • • • • • • • • • • • • • • • • • • • •

Mein Mann ist krank."

"Hat er Temperatur?"
"Ja, er hat ziemlich hohes Fieber."

Der Arzt kommt ins Zimmer. 
"Na, Herr Schmidt, wie fühlen Sie sich?"

"Ziemlich schwach,
Herr Doktor."

Der Arzt untersucht
Herrn Schmidt.

"Tut das weh?" "Nur ein
bisschen; nicht sehr."

Der Arzt legt die Hand
auf Herrn Schmidts Stirn.

Er nimmt seinen Puls

und seine Temperatur.

"Machen Sie den Mund auf!"

"Strecken Sie die Zunge heraus!  Sagen Sie ah!"

● ● ● ● ● ● ● ● ● ● ● ● ● ● ● ● ● ● ● ● ● ● ● ● ● ● ● ● ● ● ● ● ● ● ● ● ● ● ● ● ● ● ● ● ●

"Ihre Zunge ist etwas belegt.

Und Ihr Hals ist ein wenig entzündet."

"Sie haben eine Grippe. Aber es ist nicht gefährlich.

Ich gebe Ihnen eine Spritze. Das wird das Fieber herunterbringen.

Ich will Ihnen auch ein paar Pillen verschreiben.

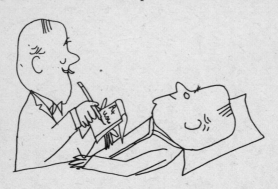

Nehmen Sie eine davon drei Mal am Tag."

"Nehmen Sie auch Nasentropfen.

Und trinken Sie viel Limonade!

• • • • • • • • • • • • • • • • • • • • • • • • • • • • • • • • • • • • • • • • • • • • • •

Vor allem brauchen Sie Ruhe. Bleiben Sie im Bett

und in ein paar Tagen sind Sie wieder in Ordnung."

Der Arzt verschreibt
die Pillen. Er gibt
Frau Schmidt das Rezept.

Frau Schmidt bringt
das Rezept zur Apotheke.

Der Apotheker verkauft Medizin.

"Kann ich dieses Rezept schnell haben?"
"Ja, Sie können darauf warten.
Es dauert nur fünf Minuten."

Herr Schmidt nimmt
die Pillen

und die Nasentropfen.

Er gurgelt.

Er trinkt heissen Tee
und kalte Limonade.

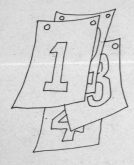

Nach ein paar Tagen
geht es ihm besser.

Er hat keine
Temperatur mehr.

Er hat keine Schmerzen.
Er ist nicht mehr blass.

Er ist wieder gesund.
Er kann wieder ins
Büro gehen.

1. Was tun Karl und Otto nach der Schule?

2. Was tut Gretchen?

3. Wohin bringt Herr Schmidt den Wagen?

4. Was tut er dann?

5. Wo ist Frau Schmidt?

6. Warum zieht Gretchen ein anderes Kleid an?

7. Wohin geht Gretchen mit ihrem Freund?

8. Wer kommt zu den Schmidts?

9. Wohin geht die Familie
am Sonntag Vormittag?

10. Wen besuchen die
Kinder am Nachmittag?

11. Warum ist Frau Schmidt
heute Abend froh?

12. Was bringt der Kellner?

13. Was bestellt Herr
Schmidt zu trinken?

14. Was gibt es
zum Nachtisch?

15. Was bringt der
Kellner nach dem Essen?

16. Warum sagt der
Kellner "Danke vielmals"?

17. Welche Instrumente hat das Orchester?

18. Wo ist Herr Schmidt?

19. Wen hat Frau Schmidt gerufen?

20. Wie oft soll Herr Schmidt die Pillen nehmen?

ANTWORTEN

1. Sie spielen Fussball mit ihren Freunden.
2. Sie liest eine Zeitschrift und spielt Schallplatten.
3. Er bringt den Wagen in die Garage.
4. Er geht ins Wohnzimmer und liest die Zeitung.
5. Sie ist in der Küche.
6. Sie hat eine Verabredung.
7. Sie gehen ins Kino.
8. Herr und Frau Müller kommen zu Besuch.
9. Sie gehen in die Kirche.
10. Sie besuchen ihre Grosseltern.
11. Die Familie geht in ein Restaurant.
    Sie braucht nicht zu kochen.
12. Er bringt die Weinkarte und die Speisekarte.
13. Herr Schmidt bestellt eine Flasche Bier.
14. Zum Nachtisch gibt es Kuchen und Eis.
15. Er bringt die Rechnung.
16. Herr Schmidt gibt ihm ein Trinkgeld.
17. Das Orchester hat ein Klavier,
    eine Geige und eine Ziehharmonika.
18. Herr Schmidt ist im Bett.
19. Frau Schmidt hat den Arzt gerufen.
20. Er soll die Pillen drei Mal am Tag nehmen.

Es ist Sommer.

Karl und Otto haben
keine Schule.
Sie haben Ferien.

Gretchen hat zwei Wochen Urlaub.
Herr Schmidt hat auch Urlaub.

Die Familie will nicht in der Stadt bleiben.
Sie wollen wegfahren.

Im Sommer fahren viele
Leute auf Reisen.

Viele Leute fahren
ans Meer.

Andere fahren in
die Berge.

Andere fahren in
fremde Länder.

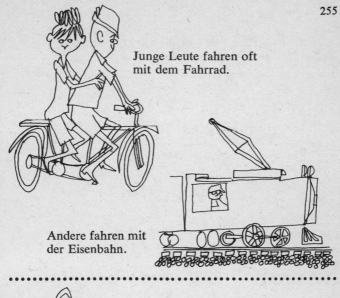

Junge Leute fahren oft
mit dem Fahrrad.

Andere fahren mit
der Eisenbahn.

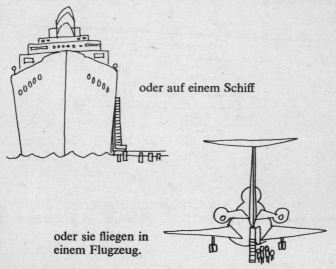

oder auf einem Schiff

oder sie fliegen in
einem Flugzeug.

Hier ist ein Flugplatz (Flughafen). Ein Flugzeug wartet.
Die Passagiere steigen ein.

Ein Flugzeug landet. Ein anderes Flugzeug fliegt ab.
Ein Hubschrauber ist in der Luft.

Hier ist ein Schiff. Es ist im Hafen. Es liegt am Pier.
Die Passagiere kommen an Bord und gehen in ihre Kabinen.

Die Familie Schmidt will aufs Land fahren.
Frau Schmidt packt die Koffer.

Endlich ist alles fertig.

Der Vater ruft ein Taxi.

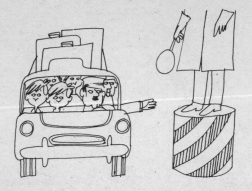

Das Taxi kommt.
Sie laden die Koffer
in den Kofferraum und auf
das Dach und steigen ein.

"Zum Bahnhof, bitte!
Fahren Sie schnell,
es ist spät!"

Hier ist der Bahnhof.

Die Familie steigt aus.
Herr Schmidt zahlt dem
Taxichauffeur und gibt
ihm ein Trinkgeld.

Ein Dienstmann (Gepäckträger) kommt.

Er lädt die Koffer auf seinen Karren.

"Die kleinen Handkoffer
können Sie mit in das
Abteil nehmen, aber
den grossen Koffer
müssen Sie aufgeben.

Ich tue es für Sie.
Ich bringe Ihnen
den Gepäckschein."

Herr Schmidt hat fünf
Fahrkarten zweiter Klasse.

Er geht zum
Auskunftsschalter.

Er kommt zurück und sagt:
"Wir haben noch ein
wenig Zeit.
Unser Zug hat
15 Minuten Verspätung.

Unser Zug geht auf
Bahnsteig sieben ab."

Die Familie geht in
den Wartesaal. Sie setzen
sich auf eine Bank
und warten.

Bald ist es Zeit.
Sie gehen zum Bahnsteig.

An der Sperre steht
ein Schaffner.

Er kontrolliert
die Fahrkarten.

Hier kommt der Zug.
Er hält. Viele Leute
steigen aus.

"Einsteigen, bitte!"
ruft der Zugführer.
Alle steigen ein.

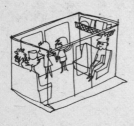

Hier ist ein Abteil
zweiter Klasse.
Die Koffer sind schon
im Gepäcknetz.

"Abfahrt!" ruft der
Zugführer. Der Zug
fährt langsam ab.

Die Fahrt ist nicht
sehr lange. Wir brauchen
keinen Schlafwagen.

Wir essen unser
Mittagessen im
Speisewagen.

Der Zug kommt an.

Wir nehmen unsere Koffer
und steigen aus.

Wir wohnen nicht in
einem Hotel. Ein Hotel
ist zu teuer.

Wir wohnen in einer
kleinen Pension.

Wir haben Zimmer mit
fliessendem Wasser,
aber ohne Badezimmer.

Das Badezimmer und
die Toilette sind
auf dem Gang.

Diese Pension ist in einem kleinen Dorf im Gebirge.

Vom Balkon haben wir eine wunderschöne Aussicht.

Wir können lange
Spaziergänge machen.

Karl und Otto können
wandern und auf
die Berge steigen.

Hier ist auch ein schöner kleiner See.

Hier können wir schwimmen

· · · · · · · · · · · · · · · · · · · · · · · · · · · · · · · · · ·

rudern                    und segeln.

Die Zeit vergeht schnell. Gestern waren wir in der Stadt.

Heute sind wir hier und schwimmen im See.

Herr Schmidt liegt in der Sonne und ruht sich aus.

Otto geht reiten.

Heute Abend spielt die
Dorfkapelle auf dem
Dorfplatz. Sie spielt
Tanzmusik. Es ist
ein Walzer.

"Darf ich um den
nächsten Tanz bitten?"
"O ja, sehr gerne!"

Morgen werden wir
Tennis spielen.

Nächste Woche wird
ein Zirkus durch
das Dorf kommen.

In zwei Wochen sind die Ferien zu Ende.

Die Familie Schmidt fährt wieder nach Hause.

● ● ● ● ● ● ● ● ● ● ● ● ● ● ● ● ● ● ● ● ● ● ● ● ● ● ● ● ● ● ● ● ● ● ● ● ● ● ● ● ● ●

Auf Wiedersehen, Herr und Frau Schmidt,
Gretchen, Karl und Otto!

Wir haben viel Deutsch von Ihnen gelernt.

# Irregular Verbs

The following table lists the 100 most important irregular German verbs. For each verb, the infinitive, the singular of the past tense, and the past participle is shown. Those verbs which form their perfect tense with the helping verb *sein* have this fact indicated by the word *ist* in parentheses before the past participle. The fourth column shows the 3rd person singular of the present tense only for those verbs which have irregularities in this form. The final column lists the English meaning.

This list does not contain the many compounds that can be formed from these verbs. All verb compounds have the same principal parts as the stem on which they are based. Thus, for example, the verbs *abnehmen, annehmen, aufnehmen, benehmen, entnehmen, mitnehmen, unternehmen, vernehmen, wegnehmen, zunehmen*, etc., all have the same form in all their tenses as the verb *nehmen*. Only *nehmen* will therefore be found in the list.

| Infinitive | Past Tense | Past Participle | Present | Meaning |
|---|---|---|---|---|
| befehlen | befahl | befohlen | befiehlt | command |
| beginnen | begann | begonnen | | begin |
| beissen | biss | gebissen | | bite |
| biegen | bog | gebogen | | bend |
| bieten | bot | geboten | | offer |
| binden | band | gebunden | | bind |
| bitten | bat | gebeten | | ask, request |
| blasen | blies | geblasen | bläst | blow |
| bleiben | blieb | (ist) geblieben | | stay |
| braten | briet | gebraten | brät | roast |
| brechen | brach | gebrochen | bricht | break |
| brennen | brannte | gebrannt | | burn |
| bringen | brachte | gebracht | | bring |

| Infinitive | Past Tense | Past Participle | Present | Meaning |
|---|---|---|---|---|
| denken | dachte | gedacht | | think |
| dürfen | durfte | gedurft | darf | be permitted |
| essen | ass | gegessen | isst | eat |
| fahren | fuhr | (ist) gefahren | fährt | drive |
| fallen | fiel | (ist) gefallen | fällt | fall |
| fangen | fing | gefangen | fängt | catch |
| finden | fand | gefunden | | find |
| fliegen | flog | (ist) geflogen | | fly |
| fliehen | floh | (ist) geflohen | | flee |
| fliessen | floss | (ist) geflossen | | flow |
| frieren | fror | gefroren | | freeze |
| geben | gab | gegeben | gibt | give |
| gehen | ging | (ist) gegangen | | go |
| gelingen | gelang | (ist) gelungen | | succeed |
| geniessen | genoss | genossen | | enjoy |
| geschehen | geschah | (ist) geschehen | geschieht | happen |
| gewinnen | gewann | gewonnen | | win |
| giessen | goss | gegossen | | pour |
| graben | grub | gegraben | gräbt | dig |
| greifen | griff | gegriffen | | grab |
| halten | hielt | gehalten | hält | hold |
| heben | hob | gehoben | | lift |
| heissen | hiess | geheissen | | be called |
| helfen | half | geholfen | hilft | help |
| kennen | kannte | gekannt | | know |
| klingen | klang | geklungen | | sound |
| kommen | kam | (ist) gekommen | | come |
| können | konnte | gekonnt | kann | can |
| laden | lud | geladen | lädt | load |
| lassen | liess | gelassen | lässt | let |
| laufen | lief | (ist) gelaufen | läuft | run |
| leiden | litt | gelitten | | suffer |
| lesen | las | gelesen | liest | read |
| liegen | lag | gelegen | | lie (lay, lain) |
| lügen | log | gelogen | | lie (lied) |
| messen | mass | gemessen | misst | measure |

| Infinitive | Past Tense | Past Participle | Present | Meaning |
|---|---|---|---|---|
| mögen | mochte | gemocht | mag | may, like |
| müssen | musste | gemusst | muss | must |
| nehmen | nahm | genommen | nimmt | take |
| nennen | nannte | genannt | | name |
| pfeifen | pfiff | gepfiffen | | whistle |
| raten | riet | geraten | rät | guess, advise |
| reiten | ritt | (ist) geritten | | ride |
| rennen | rannte | (ist) gerannt | | run |
| riechen | roch | gerochen | | smell |
| rufen | rief | gerufen | | call |
| scheinen | schien | geschienen | | shine, seem |
| schieben | schob | geschoben | | shove |
| schiessen | schoss | geschossen | | shoot |
| schlafen | schlief | geschlafen | schläft | sleep |
| schlagen | schlug | geschlagen | schlägt | hit |
| schliessen | schloss | geschlossen | | close |
| schneiden | schnitt | geschnitten | | cut |
| schreiben | schrieb | geschrieben | | write |
| schreien | schrie | geschrieen | | shout |
| schweigen | schwieg | geschwiegen | | be silent |
| schwimmen | schwamm | (ist) geschwommen | | swim |
| sehen | sah | gesehen | sieht | see |
| sein | war | (ist) gewesen | ist | be |
| senden | sandte | gesandt | | send |
| singen | sang | gesungen | | sing |
| sinken | sank | (ist) gesunken | | sink |
| sitzen | sass | gesessen | | sit |
| sprechen | sprach | gesprochen | spricht | speak |
| springen | sprang | (ist) gesprungen | | jump |
| stehen | stand | gestanden | | stand |
| stehlen | stahl | gestohlen | stiehlt | steal |
| steigen | stieg | (ist) gestiegen | | climb |
| sterben | starb | (ist) gestorben | stirbt | die |
| stossen | stiess | gestossen | stösst | shove |
| streiten | stritt | gestritten | | argue |
| tragen | trug | getragen | trägt | carry |
| treffen | traf | getroffen | trifft | meet |
| treiben | trieb | getrieben | | drive, carry on |
| treten | trat | getreten | tritt | step |

| *Infinitive* | *Past Tense* | *Past Participle* | *Present* | *Meaning* |
|---|---|---|---|---|
| trinken | trank | getrunken | | drink |
| tun | tat | getan | | do |
| vergessen | vergass | vergessen | vergisst | forget |
| verlieren | verlor | verloren | | lose |
| wachsen | wuchs | (ist) gewaschen | wächst | grow |
| waschen | wusch | gewaschen | wäscht | wash |
| werden | wurde (ward) | (ist) geworden | wird | become |
| werfen | warf | geworfen | wirft | throw |
| wiegen | wog | gewogen | | weigh |
| wissen | wusste | gewusst | weiss | know |
| wollen | wollte | gewollt | will | want |
| ziehen | zog | gezogen | | pull |

# Vocabulary

This vocabulary is complete; it contains all the words that occur in the text, as well as in the pronunciation guide and the grammar section. For each word, only the meaning in which it is used in this book is listed.

Compounds, derivatives, and idiomatic phrases are listed under the main entry; if they involve more than one word, they are cross-indexed.

Numerals are listed only as they occur in the text.

Adjectives are shown in their stem form, without endings. They are therefore identical with the corresponding adverbs. Comparative and superlative forms are listed if they occur in the text.

Each noun is listed with its article, followed by an indication of its plural form. A dash (—) indicates that the plural has no ending; otherwise the ending is shown. If the plural of the noun takes an *Umlaut*, this is shown by the sign ¨ over the dash; thus, *der Vater*, ¨ means that the plural is *die Väter; die Hand*, ¨e means that the plural is *die Hände*. The *Umlaut* is placed on the first vowel of the stem: *das Haus*, ¨er: *die Häuser*. In a compound noun, only the last part will take the *Umlaut: der Briefkasten*, ¨: *die Briefkästen*.

For irregular verbs, the principal parts are given: *singen, sang, hat gesungen*. If the verb takes the helping verb *sein*, this is indicated as follows: *kommen, kam, ist gekommen* or *aufwachen (ist)*. Verbs that have an irregularity in the present tense, have this form listed after a semicolon: *lesen, las, hat gelesen; liest*. In addition, the present tense form is also listed in its own alphabetic sequence. Verbs with separable prefixes have a raised dot between the prefix and the stem: *auf·stehen*.

# A

**ab** — off, from
**der Abend –e** — evening
**das Abendessen, – –** — supper
**aber** — but
**ab·fahren, fuhr ab, ist abgefahren; fährt ab** — to depart
**Abfahrt!** — all aboard!
**ab·fliegen, flog ab, ist abgeflogen** — to take off (airplane)
**ab·hängen** — to hang up (telephone)
**ab·holen** — to call for someone
**ab·legen** — to put down (clothes)
**ab·nehmen, nahm ab, hat abgenommen; nimmt ab** — to take off
**ab·schliessen, schloss ab, hat abgeschlossen** — to lock
**ab·stauben** — to dust
**das Abteil, –e** — compartment
**die Abteilung, –en** — department
**ach!** — alas!
**acht** — eight; **achtundzwanzig** — 28; **achtzehn** — 18; **achtzig** — 80
**die Adresse, –n** — address
**alle** — all; **vor allem** — above all; **alles** — everything
**als** — as, than, when
**alt, älter, am ältesten** — old, older, oldest
**am** — at the, on the
**Amerika** — America; **der Amerikaner, – –** American; **amerikanisch** — American
**an** — at, on
**andere** — other
**anderes, anders** — different
**an·fangen, fing an, hat angefangen; fängt an** — to begin
**an·halten, hielt an, hat angehalten; hält an** — to stop, to hold on
**an·kommen, kam an, ist angekommen** — to arrive
**an·rufen, rief an, hat angerufen** — to telephone
**ans** — to the
**anstatt** — instead of
**antworten** — to answer
**an·ziehen, zog an, hat angezogen** — to put on (clothes), to dress; **sich an·ziehen** — to get dressed
**der Anzug, ⁼e** — suit
**der Apéritif, –s** — cocktail
**der Apfel, ⁼** — apple
**die Apotheke, –n** — pharmacy; **der Apotheker, –** pharmacist

**April** — April
**die Arbeit, –en** — work; **arbeiten** — to work; **der Arbeitstag, –e** — working day
**der Arm, –e** — arm; **die Armbanduhr, –en** — wrist watch
**der Arzt, ⁼e** — doctor
**der Aschenbecher, – –** — ashtray
**auch** — also
**auf** — on, open
**die Aufgabe, –n** — assignment
**auf·geben, gab auf, hat aufgegeben; gibt auf** — to deliver, to give up
**auf·gehen, ging auf, ist aufgegangen** — to rise (sun)
**auf·hängen** — to hang up
**auf·machen** — to open
**aufs** — to the
**der Aufschnitt, –e (kalter A.)** — cold cuts
**auf·stehen, stand auf, ist aufgestanden** — to stand up, to get up
**auf·tragen, trug auf, hat aufgetragen; trägt auf** — to put on, apply
**auf·wachen (ist)** — to wake up
**der Aufzug, ⁼e** — elevator
**das Auge, –n** — eye
**August** — August
**aus** — out of
**aus·gehen, gingaus, ist ausgegangen** — to go out
**der Auskunftsschalter, – –** — information desk
**aus·löschen** — to put out, extinguish
**(sich) aus·ruhen** — to relax
**die Aussicht, –en** — view
**aus·steigen, stieg aus, ist ausgestiegen** — get off
**die Austellung, –en** — exhibition
**(sich) aus·ziehen, zog aus, hat ausgezogen** — to undress
**das Auto, –s** — automobile
**der Autobus, –se** — bus
**der Automat, –en** — automat

# B

**der Bäcker** — baker
**die Badewanne, –n** — bathtub; **das Badezimmer** — bathroom
**der Bahnhof, ⁼e** — train station; **der Bahnsteig, –e** — platform
**bald** — soon
**der Balkon, –e** — balcony

der Ball, ⸚e — ball
die Banane, –n — banana
die Bank, ⸚e — bench
der Bär, –en — bear
die Bar, –s — bar
die Batterie, –n — battery
der Baum, ⸚e — tree
beginnen, begann, hat begonnen —
to begin
bei — at, near, with
das Bein, –e — leg
bekommen, bekam, hat bekommen
— to get, receive
belegt — coated
das Benzin — gasoline
der Berg, –e — mountain
besetzt — busy, occupied
besser — better
bestellen — to order
der Besuch, –e — visit, company; besuchen — to visit; der Besucher —
guest, visitor
betrunken — drunk
das Bett, –en — bed; die Bettwäsche
— bed linen
bevor — before
das Bier — beer
das Bild, –er — picture
billig — cheap
bin — (I) am
die Birne, –n — pear
bis — until
ein bisschen — a little
bitte — please
bitten, bat, hat gebeten (um) — to
ask (for)
blasen, blies, hat geblasen; bläst —
to blow
blass — pale
das Blatt, ⸚er — leaf
blau — blue
bleiben, blieb, ist geblieben — to remain, stay
der Bleistift, –e — pencil
die Blume, –n — flower
die Bluse, –n — blouse
die Bohne, –n — bean
das Boot, –e — boat
an Bord — on board
der Braten, – — roast; die Bratwurst,
⸚e — sausage
brauchen — to need
braun — brown
die Brause, –n — shower
der Brief, –e — letter; der Briefkasten, ⸚ — mailbox; die Briefmarke,

–n — stamp; der Briefträger —
mailman; der Briefumschlag, ⸚e
— envelope
bringen, brachte, hat gebracht — to
bring
das Brot, –e — bread; das Brötchen
— roll
der Bruder, ⸚ — brother
das Buch, ⸚er — book; das Bücherbrett, –er — bookshelf
das Bügelbrett, –er — ironing board;
das Bügeleisen, – — iron; bügeln —
to iron
bunt — colorful
das Büro, –s — office
bürsten — to brush
der Busch, ⸚e — bush
der Büstenhalter, – — brassiere
die Butter — butter; das Butterbrot,
–e — sandwich

## C

das Café, –s — café
das Cello, –s — cello
das Chaos — chaos
der Chauffeur, –e — chauffeur
die Crème, –n — cream

## D

da — there, here, since
das Dach, ⸚er — roof
die Dame, –n — lady; die Damen-
kleider — ladies' clothing
damit — so that; with it
danke — thanks; danke vielmals,
danke sehr, danke schön — thank
you very much; danken — to thank
dann — then
darauf — for that
darf — may (see dürfen)
das — the, that
dass — that
dauern — to last, take time
der Daumen — thumb
davon — of that, of them
die Decke, –n — blanket, cover, ceil-
ing
decken — to cover; den Tisch decken
— to set the table
dein — your
dem — the, to the, to whom, to which

**den** — the, whom, which
**denen** — to whom, to which
**denken, dachte, hat gedacht** — to think
**denn** — for
**der** — the, who, which
**deren** — of which
**des** — of the
**dessen** — of which
**deutsch** — German; **der Deutsche, –n** – a German; **Deutschland** — Germany
**Dezember** — December
**dich** — you
**dick** — thick, fat
**die** — the
**dienen** — to serve; **womit kann ich dienen?** — Can I help you? What can I do for you?
**Dienstag** — Tuesday
**der Dienstmann, ⁼er**—porter
**dies** — this
**diesmal** — this time
**diktieren** — to dictate
**das Ding, -e** – thing
**dir** — to you
**der Doktor, –en** – doctor
**Donnerstag** — Thursday
**das Dorf, ⁼er** – village; **die Dorfkapelle, –n** – village band; **der Dorfplatz, ⁼e** – village square
**dort** — there
**drei** — three; **dreissig** — thirty; **dreiundzwanzig** — twenty-three; **dreizehn** — thirteen; **dritter** — third
**du** — you
**dumm** — stupid
**dunkel** — dark
**durch** — through
**dürfen, durfte, gedurft; darf** — to be permitted, be allowed, may
**durstig** — thirsty
**das Dutzend, -e** – dozen

**E**

**das Ei, -er** – egg
**der Eifer** — zeal
**ein** — a, an, one
**eingeschrieben** — registered
**ein·kaufen** — to shop; **die Einkaufstasche, –n** – shopping bag
**einmal** — once; **noch einmal** — once again, once more
**ein·packen** — to pack

**eins** — one
**ein·schlafen, schlief ein, ist eingeschlafen; schläft ein** – to fall asleep
**ein·steigen, stieg ein, ist eingestiegen** — to get in
**einunddreissig** — thirty-one
**einundzwanzig** — twenty-one
**einverstanden** — agreed
**das Eis** — ice, ice cream
**die Eisenbahn, -en** – railroad
**die Eisenwaren** — hardware
**der Eiskasten** — refrigerator
**elektrisch** — electric
**elf** — eleven
**die Eltern** — parents
**das Ende** — end; **zu Ende sein** — to be at an end; **endlich** – finally
**England** — England; **der Engländer, – –** Englishman; **Englisch** – English
**entlang** — along
**entschuldigen** — to pardon; **Entschuldigen Sie!** – pardon me!
**entzündet** — inflamed
**er** — he, it
**Die Erbse, -n** – pea
**das Erdgeschoss** — ground floor
**die Erkältung, -en** – cold
**erklären** — to explain
**erlaubt** — allowed, permitted
**erst** — first
**erzählen** — to tell
**es** — it
**essen, ass, hat gegessen; isst** — to eat
**der Essig** — vinegar
**etwas** — something
**euch** — you; **euer** — your
**Europa** — Europe
**das Examen, – –** test

**F**

**die Fahne, -n** – flag
**fahren, fuhr, ist gefahren; fährt** — to drive, ride; **die Fahrkarte, –n** – ticket; **das Fahrrad, ⁼er** – bicycle; **die Fahrt, –en** – trip; **fährt ab** – departs; **fährt weg** – drives off
**fallen, fiel, ist gefallen; fällt** — to fall
**falsch** — wrong
**die Familie, –n** – family
**die Farbe, –n** – color
**Februar** — February

die Feder, –n — pen
das Feld, –er — field
das Fenster — window
die Ferien — vacation
das Fernsehprogramm, –e — television program
fertig — ready
der Feuerwehrwagen, – – fire engine
das Feuerzeug, –e — cigarette lighter
das Fieber — fever
die Figur, –en — figure
der Film, –e — film
finden, fand, hat gefunden — to find
der Finger, – – finger
der Fisch, –e — fish
die Flasche, –n — bottle
das Fleisch — meat; der Fleischer — butcher
fleissig — diligently
fliegen, flog, ist geflogen — to fly; fliegt ab — takes off
fliessend — flowing, running (water)
der Flughafen, ̈; der Flugplatz, ̈e — airport; das Flugzeug, –e — airplane
folgen (ist) — to follow
die Frage, –n — question; fragen — to ask
die Frau, –en — woman, wife, Mrs.
das Fräulein — young lady, Miss
Freitag — Friday
fremd — foreign
sich freuen — to be happy; es freut mich — I am glad
der Freund, –e — friend; die Freundin, –nen — girl friend
frisch — fresh
froh — happy
der Fruchtsaft, ̈e — fruit juice
der Frühling — spring
das Frühstück, –e — breakfast; das Frühstücksgeschirr — breakfast dishes; der Frühstückstisch, –e — breakfast table
der Fuchs, ̈e — fox
fühlen — to feel
führen — to lead
füllen — to fill
fünf — five; der Fünfmarkschein, –e — five mark bill; fünfundfünfzig — fifty-five; fünfundvierzig — forty-five; fünfzehn — fifteen; fünfzig — fifty; das Fünfzigpfennigstück, –e — 50-pfennig piece
für —for

der Fuss, ̈e — foot; zu Fuss — on foot; der Fussball, ̈e — soccer ball; das Fussballspiel, –e — soccer game; der Fussboden, ̈ — floor; die Fussbremse, –n — foot brake; die Fussmatte, –n — doormat

# G

die Gabel, –n — fork
gähnen — to yawn
der Gang, ̈e — hallway
ganz — whole, quite
die Garage, –n — garage; die Garagetür, –en — garage door
die Garderobe, –n — cloakroom
der Garten, ̈ — garden
das Gas, –e — gas; der Gashebel — gas pedal, accelerator
geben, gab, hat gegeben; gibt — to give; es gibt — there is
das Gebirge, – – mountains
gefährlich — dangerous
das Geflügel — poultry
gegen — against; gegenüber — opposite
gehen, ging, ist gegangen — to go; geht aus — goes out; wie geht's? Wie geht es Ihnen? — how are you?; es geht ihm besser — he feels better
gehören — to belong
die Geige, –n — violin
gelb — yellow
das Geld, –er — money
gelernt — learned (see lernen)
das Gemüse, – – vegetables; die Gemüsefrau, –en — vegetable woman; der Gemüsehändler, – – greengrocer
das Genie, –s — genius
genug — enough
das Gepäck — luggage; das Gepäcknetz, – – luggage rack; der Gepäckschein, –e — luggage receipt; der Gepäckträger, – – porter
geradeaus — straight ahead
gern — gladly; sehr gern — with pleasure
das Geschäft, –e — office, business, store; der Geschäftsfreund, –e — business acquaintance; das Geschäftshaus, ̈er — office building
geschehen, geschah, ist geschehen; geschieht — to happen

das Geschenk, -e — gift, present
die Geschichte, -n — story
das Geschirr — dishes
das Gesicht, -er — face
das Gespräch, -e — conversation
gestern — yesterday
gesund — healthy
gewöhnlich — ordinary, usual
das Gewürz, -e — spice
gibt — gives (see geben); es gibt — there is, there are
das Glas, ⸚er — glass; das Glashaus, ⸚er —glass house
das Glück — luck, happiness; Glück haben — to be lucky; glücklich — happy
die Gnade, -n — grace
golden — golden; das Gold — gold
das Grammophon, -e — phonograph
das Gras, ⸚er — grass
die Grippe — grippe, flu
gross, grösser, am grössten — big, bigger, biggest
die Grosseltern — grandparents; die Grossmutter, ⸚ — grandmother; der Grossvater, ⸚ — grandfather
grün — green
gurgeln — to gargle
der Gürtel, — belt
gut, besser, am besten — good, better, best; guten Morgen! — good morning! guten Tag! — good day!

**H**

das Haar, -e — hair
haben, hatte, hat gehabt — to have
der Hafen, ⸚ — harbor
halb — half; halb drei — half past two
hallo! — hello!
der Hals, ⸚ — neck; die Halsschmerzen — sore throat
halten, hielt, hat gehalten; hält — to hold, stop; hält an — stops
das Hammelfleisch — mutton
die Hand, ⸚e — hand; die Handbremse, -n — hand brake; der Handkoffer, — — suitcase; der Handschuh, -e — glove; die Handtasche, -n — pocketbook, handbag; das Handtuch, ⸚er — towel
hängt ab, hängt auf — hangs up
hat — has (see haben)
die Haube, -n — hood

die Hauptstadt, ⸚e — capital city
das Haus, ⸚er — house; die Haushaltartikel — household goods; die Haustür, -en — front door; nach Hause — home(ward); zu Hause — at home
heben, hob, hat gehoben — to raise
das Heft, -e — notebook
heiser — hoarse
heiss — hot
heissen, hiess, hat geheissen — to be called; ich heisse . . . — my name is . . . ; wie heissen Sie? — what's your name?
helfen, half, hat geholfen; hilft — to help
das Hemd, -en — shirt
her — here, in this direction
der Herbst — autumn
der Herd, -e — kitchen stove, range
herein! — come in!
herein·kommen, kam herein, ist hereingekommen — to come in
der Hering, -e — herring
der Herr, -en — man, gentleman, master, Mr.
herunter·bringen, brachte herunter, hat heruntergebracht — to bring down
heute — today; heute Abend — this evening, tonight
hier — here
hilft — helps (see helfen)
hinter — behind
hoch, hoher — high; höher — higher; am höchsten — highest
holen — to get, fetch
die Hölle — hell
hören — to hear, listen
die Hose, -n — pants
das Hotel, -s — hotel
hübsch — pretty
der Hubschrauber, - — helicopter
das Huhn, ⸚er — chicken
der Hund, -e — dog
hundert — hundred
hungrig — hungry
husten — to cough
der Hut, ⸚e — hat

**I**

ich — I
ihm — him, to him, to it
ihn — him, it
ihnen — to them

Ihnen — to you
ihr — her, to her, their; you
Ihr — your
im — in the
immer — always
in — in, into
ins — into the
das Instrument, -e — instrument; das Instrumentenbrett, -er — dashboard
interessant — interesting
ist — is (see sein)
isst — eats (see essen)

## J

ja — yes
die Jacke, -n — jacket
das Jahr, -e — year; die Jahreszeit, -en — season
Januar — January
jeder — each, every
jener — that, those
jetzt — now
Juli — July
jung, jünger, der jüngste — young, younger, the youngest
der Junge, -n — boy, youngster
Juni Juno

## K

die Kabine, -n — cabin
der Kaffee — coffee; die Kaffeekanne -n — coffee pot
das Kalbfleisch — veal
kalt — cold
kämmen — to comb
der Kanarienvogel, ¨ — canary
kann — can (see können)
die Kappe, -n — cap
die Karotte, -n — carrot
der Karren, - — cart
die Karte, -n — card
die Kartoffel, -n — potato
der Käse, - — cheese; das Käsebrot, -e — cheese sandwich
die Kasse, -n — cash register
die Katze, -n — cat
kaufen — to buy
kegeln gehen — to go bowling
kein — no, none, not a, not any
der (das) Keks, -e — cookie

der Kellner, - — waiter
das Kind, -er — child
das Kino, -s — movie theater
die Kirche, -n — church
die Kirsche, -n — cherry
die Klasse, -n — class; das Klassenzimmer, - — classroom
das Klavier, -e — piano
das Kleid, -er — dress
die Kleider — clothes
klein — small; das Kleingeld — change
die Klingel, -n — doorbell
klopfen — to knock
das Knie, -e — knee
der Knödel, - — dumpling
kochen — to cook
der Koffer, - — suitcase; der Kofferraum — trunk (of a car)
der Kohl — cabbage
der Kolonialwarenhändler, - — grocer
kommen, kam, ist gekommen — to come
die Kommode, -n — chest of drawers
kommt an — arrives (see ankommen)
können, konnte, gekonnt; kann — can, to be able
kontrollieren — to check, control
das Konzert, -e — concert
der Kopf, ¨e — head; die Kopfschmerzen — headache
der Körper, - — body; der Körperteil, -e — part of the body
kosten — to cost
das Kostüm, -e — ladies' suit
der Kotflügel, - — fender
krank — sick; die Krankheit, -en — sickness
die Kreide — chalk
die Kreuzung, -en — street crossing
der Kronleuchter, - — chandelier
die Küche, -n — kitchen; der Küchenschrank, ¨e — kitchen cabinet; der Küchentisch, -e — kitchen table
der Kuchen, - — cake
die Kuckucksuhr, -en — cuckoo clock
der Kühler, - — car radiator
der Kühlschranke, ¨e — refrigerator
der Kunde, -n — customer
die Kupplung, -en — clutch
kurz — short
die Kurzwaren — haberdashery, notions

# L

**laden, lud, hat geladen; lädt** — to load
**der Laden, ⸚** — store
**die Lampe, –n** — lamp
**das Land, ⸚er** — country; **aufs Land** — to the country; **landen** — to land; **die Landkarte, –n** — map
**lang, länger** — long, longer
**langsam** — slow
**lassen, liess, hat gelassen; lässt** — to let
**der Lastwagen, – –** — truck
**laufen, lief, ist gelaufen; läuft** — to run
**laut** — loud
**läuten** — to ring
**die Leberpastete, –n** — chopped liver, liver paté; **die Leberwurst** — liverwurst
**leer** — empty
**(sich) legen** — to lie down; **legt ab** — puts down (see **ablegen**)
**der Lehrer, – –** — teacher
**leicht** — easy
**leise** — soft
**das Lenkrad, ⸚er** — steering wheel
**lernen** — to learn
**lesen, las, hat gelesen; liest** — to read
**die Leute** — people
**das Licht, –er** — light
**lieben** — to love
**lieber** — rather
**liegen, lag, hat gelegen** — to lie
**liest** — reads (see **lesen**)
**der Liftjunge, –n** — elevator boy
**die Limonade, –n** — lemonade
**links** — left
**die Lippe, –n** — lip
**die Liste, –n** — list
**der Liter, – –** — approx. one quart
**der Löffel, – –** — spoon
**löscht aus** — puts out (the light) (see **auslöschen**)
**der Löwe, –n** — lion
**die Luft, ⸚e** — air; **die Luftpostmarke, –n** — airmail stamp
**lyrisch** — lyrical

# M

**machen** — to make
**das Mädchen, – –** — girl
**mag** — likes, may (see **mögen**)

**Mai** — May
**der Mais** — corn
**das Mal** — time; **drei Mal** — three times
**man** — one, a person
**manchmal** — sometimes
**der Mann, ⸚er** — man, husband; **Männerkleider** — men's clothing
**der Mantel, ⸚** — overcoat
**die Mark** — German unit of currency; **das Markstück, –e** — one-mark piece, about 25¢
**die Marmelade, –n** — jam
**März** — March
**die Matte, –n** — bathmat
**die Medizin, –en** — medicine
**das Meer, –e** — ocean, sea
**mehr** — more
**mein** — my
**meist** — most
**das Messer – –** — knife
**mich** — me
**die Milch** — milk; **die Milchflasche, –n** — milk bottle; **der Milchladen, ⸚** — dairy store
**die Minute, –n** — minute
**mir** — me, to me
**mit** — with
**miteinander** — with each other
**der Mittag** — noon; **das Mittagessen, – –** — lunch; **die Mittagspause, –n** — noon recess
**die Mitternacht, ⸚e** — midnight
**Mittwoch** — Wednesday
**der Mixer, – –** — bartender
**die Möbel** — furniture
**möchte** — would like
**mögen, mochte, hat gemocht; mag** — to like, may
**der Monat, –e** — month
**der Mond, –e** — moon
**Montag** — Monday
**morgen** — tomorrow
**der Morgen, – –** — morning
**der Motor, –en** — motor
**müde** — tired
**der Mund, –e** or **⸚er** — mouth
**das Museum, die Museen** — museum
**müssen** — to have to
**die Mutter, ⸚** — mother
**die Mütze, –n** — cap

# N

**na** — well

nach — after, towards; **nach Hause** — home (ward)

nachdem — after

der Nachmittag, –e — afternoon

die Nachrichten — news

nächst — next

die Nacht, ⸚e — night; **der Nachttisch, –e** — night table

der Nachtisch, –e — dessert

nähren — to nourish

das Nähzeug — sewing utensils

der Name, –n — name; **das Namensschild, –er** — name plate

die Nase, –n — nose; **die Nasentropfen** — nose drops

nass — wet

die Nation, –en — nation

natürlich — naturally

neben — next to

nehmen, nahm, hat genommen; nimmt — to take

nein — no

das Nest, –er — nest

das Netz, –e — net

neun — nine; **neunundzwanzig** — twenty-nine; **neunzehn** — nineteen; **neunzig** — ninety

nicht — not

nichts — nothing

nie — never

nieder — down

niemand — nobody

niessen — to sneeze

nimmt — takes (see nehmen); **nimmt ab** — takes off (see abnehmen)

noch — still; **noch nicht** — not yet

November — November

die Nummer, –n — number; **das Nummernschild, –er** — license plate

nun — now

nur — only

die Nuss, ⸚e — nut

## O

ob — whether, if

oben — on top

der Ober — waiter

obgleich — although

das Obst — fruit

obwohl — although

oder — or

offen — open

öffentlich — public

öffnen — to open

oft — often

ohne — without

das Ohr, –en — ear

Oktober — October

das Öl — oil

das Orchester, – – — orchestra

die Ordnung — order

Ostdeutschland — East Germany

Österreich — Austria; **der Österreicher, – –** — Austrian

## P

ein paar — a few

das Paar, –e — pair

packen — to pack

das Paket, –e — package

das Papier, –e — paper

der Park, –e — park

parken — to park; **der Parkplatz, ⸚e** — parking place

der Passagier, –e — passenger

die Pelzjacke, –n — fur jacket

die Pension, –en — boardinghouse

die Person, –en — person

der Pfeffer — pepper

die Pfeife, –en — pipe

der Pfennig, –e — German coin, about ¼¢

das Pferd, –e — horse

die Pflanze, –n — plant

das Pfund, –e — pound

die Photographie, –en — photograph

der Pier, –e — pier

die Pille, –n — pill

der Pilz, –e — mushroom

die Pistole, –n — pistol

plätten — to iron

der Polizist, –en — policeman

der Polster, ⸚ — pillow

die Post — mail; **zur Post bringen** — to mail; **das Postamt, ⸚er** — post office; **die Postanweisung, –en** — money order; **der Postbeamte, –n** — post-office employee

der Preis, –e — price

der Professor, –en — professor

die Prüfung, –en — test

der Puls, –e — pulse

das Pult, –e — desk

die Puppe, –n — doll

putzen — to brush, polish; **sich die Zähne putzen** — to brush one's teeth

## Q

die Quelle, –n — source

## R

das Radio, –s — radio
der Rasierapparat, –e — razor
sich rasieren — to shave
die Rasierseife, –n — shaving cream
das Rathaus, ⁔er — city hall
rauchen — to smoke
die Rechnung, –en — bill
rechts — right
der Regen — rain; regnen — to rain
reich — rich
der Reifen, – – tire
rein — clean; reinigen — to clean
die Reise, –n — trip
reiten — to ride (on horseback)
die Republik, –en — republic
das Restaurant, –s — restaurant
das Rezept, –e — prescription
das Rindfleisch — beef
der Rock, ⁔e — coat; skirt
rollen — to roll; die Rolltreppe, –n
— escalator
die Rose, –n — rose
rot — red
das Rouge — rouge
rudern — to row
rufen, rief, hat gerufen — to call;
ruft an — calls up (see anrufen)
die Ruhe — rest; ruhen — to rest;
ruht sich aus — relaxes (see aus-
ruhen)

## S

sagen — to say
die Sahne — cream
der Salat, –e — salad, lettuce
das Salz — salt
Samstag — Saturday
der Satz, ⁔e — sentence
der Sauerbraten — pickled beef
das Sauerkraut — sauerkraut
die Schachtel, –n — box
der Schaffner, – – conductor
die Schallplatte, –n — record
der Schalter, – – counter
der Schalthebel, – – gear shift
scharf — sharp
der Scheibenwischer, – – windshield
wiper

der Schein, –e — bill
scheinen, schien, hat geschienen —
to shine, seem
der Scheinwerfer, – – headlight
schicken — to send
das Schiff, –e — ship
der Schillerplatz — Schiller Square
der Schinken, – — ham
schlafen, schlief, hat geschlafen;
schläft — to sleep; schläft ein —
falls asleep (see einschlafen); der
Schlafwagen, – – Pullman car;
das Schlafzimmer, – – bedroom
Schlange stehen — to stand in line
schliessen, schloss, hat geschlossen
— to close, lock
der Schlips, –e — tie
schmecken — to taste
der Schmerz, –en — pain
(sich) schminken — to put on makeup
der Schnee — snow
schneiden, schnitt, hat geschnitten —
to cut
schneien — to snow
schnell — quickly
der Schnupfen — cold in the nose
schon — already
schön — nice, pleasant, beautiful;
sich schön machen — to make
oneself look beautiful
schreiben, schrieb, hat geschrieben —
to write; die Schreibmaschine, –n
typewriter; der Schreibtisch, –e —
desk; die Schreibwaren — station-
ery
der Schuh, –e — shoe
die Schule, –n — school; die Schul-
aufgabe, –n — homework; das
Schulbuch, ⁔er — school book;
der Schüler, – — pupil
die Schulter, –n — shoulder
schwach — weak
schwarz — black
das Schweinefleisch — pork; das
Schweinskotelett, –en — pork chop
die Schweiz — Switzerland; der
Schweizer, – – Swiss
schwer — difficult, hard; heavy
die Schwester, –n — sister
schwimmen, schwamm, ist ge-
schwommen — to swim
sechs — six; sechzehn — sixteen;
sechzig — sixty
der See, –n — lake
segeln — to sail

sehen, sah, hat gesehen; sieht —to see

sehr — very

die Seife, –n — soap

sein — his

sein, war, ist gewesen; ist — to be

seit, seitdem — since

die Seite, –n — side, page

die Sekretärin, –nen — secretary

die Sekunde, –n — second

selbst — self

die Semmel, –n — roll

September — September

die Serviette, –n — napkin

der Sessel, – — armchair

sich setzen — to sit down

sich — himself, herself, itself, yourself, themselves

Sie — you

sie — she, her, it, they, them

sieben — seven; siebzehn — seventeen; siebzig — seventy

sieht — sees (see sehen)

das Signal, –e — signal

sind — are

singen, sang, hat gesungen — to sing

sitzen, sass, hat gesessen — to sit

so — as, so, thus; so . . . wie — as . . . as

die Socken — socks

das Sofa, –s — sofa

der Sohn, ⁣ꭗe — son

sollen — to be supposed to, shall, should, ought to

der Sommer — summer

sondern — but rather, but on the contrary

Sonnabend — Saturday

die Sonne, –n — sun

Sonntag — Sunday

sonst — besides, otherwise; sonst noch etwas? — anything else?

das Souterrain — basement level

spät — late; wie spät ist es? — what time is it?

spazieren gehen — go for a walk; der Spaziergang — walk

der Speck — bacon

die Speisekarte, –n — menu; der Speisewagen, – — dining car; das Speisezimmer, – — dining room

die Sperre, –n — gate

der Spiegel, – — mirror

das Spiegelei, –er — fried egg

das Spiel, –e — game; spielen — to play; der Spielplatz, ⁣ꭗe — playground; die Spielsachen, das Spielzeug — toys

sprechen, sprach, hat gesprochen; spricht — to speak

springen, sprang, ist gesprungen — to jump

die Spritze, –n — injection

der Spültisch, –e — kitchen sink

die Stadt, ⁣ꭗe — city

statt — instead of

der Staubsauger — vacuum cleaner

staubt ab — dusts (see abstauben)

stehen, stand, hat gestanden — to stand; steht auf– — get up– (see aufstehen)

die Stehlampe, –n — floor lamp

steigen, stieg, ist gestiegen — to climb; steigt aus — gets off (see aussteigen); steigt ein — gets in (see einsteigen)

der Stein, –e — stone

stellen — to put, stand

sterben, starb, ist gestorben; stirbt — to die

der Stern, –e — star

die Stirn, –en — forehead

der Stock, ⁣ꭗe — floor, story; der erste Stock — 2nd floor; der zweite Stock — 3rd floor

der Stoff, –e — material

das Stopplicht, –er — taillight

die Stosstange, –n — bumper

die Strasse, –n — street; die Strassenbahn, –en — streetcar

strecken — to extend, stretch

das Streichholz, ⁣ꭗer — match

der Strumpf, ⁣ꭗe — stocking

das Stück, –e — piece

der Student, –en — student; studieren — to study

der Stuhl, ⁣ꭗe — chair

die Stunde, –n — hour

suchen — to look for

die Suppe, –n — soup

## T

die Tafel, –n — blackboard

der Tag, –e — day

die Tankstelle, –n — gas station; der Tankwart — gas station attendant

der Tanz, ⁣ꭗe — dance; tanzen — to dance; die Tanzmusik — dance music die Tasche, -n — pocket; das Taschentuch, ⸚er — handkerchief; die Taschenuhr, -en — pocket watch

die Tasse, -n — cup

das Taxi, -s — taxi

der Taxichauffeur, -e — taxi driver

der Tee — tea

das Telefon — telephone; der Telefonanruf, -e — telephone call; das Telefonbuch, ⸚er — phone book

das Telegramm, -e — telegram

der Teller, - — plate

die Temperatur, -en — temperature

Tennis — tennis

der Teppich, -e — carpet

teuer — expensive

das Theater, - — theater

tippen — to type

der Tisch, -e — table; die Tischlampe, -n — table lamp; das Tischtuch, ⸚er — tablecloth; den Tisch decken — to set the table

die Tochter, ⸚ — daughter

die Toilette, -n — toilet; der Toiletteartikel, - — toilet article; der Toilettentisch, -e — dressing table

die Tomate, -n — tomato

das Tor, -e — gate

die Torte, -n — cake, pastry

tragen, trug, hat getragen; trägt — to carry

die Traube, -n — grape

die Treppe, -n — step, stairs

trinken, trank, hat getrunken — to drink; das Trinkgeld, -er — tip

trocknen — to dry

trotz — in spite of

tun, tat, hat getan — to do

die Tür, -en — door

# U

über — over

die Übung, -en — practice, exercise

die Uhr, -en — watch, clock; es ist sechs Uhr — it is six o'clock; wieviel Uhr ist es? — what time is it?

um — around, at

der Umlaut, -e — vowel modification

sich um·ziehen, zog sich um, hat sich umgezogen — to change clothes

und — and

die Universität, -en — university

uns — us

unser — our

unter — under

unter·gehen, ging unter, ist untergegangen — to set (sun, moon)

(sich) unterhalten, unterhielt, hat unterhalten; unterhält — to converse, entertain, enjoy oneself

das Unterhemd, -en — undershirt

die Unterhose, -n — underpants

der Unterrock, ⸚e — slip

unterschreiben, unterschrieb, hat unterschrieben — to sign

untersuchen — to examine

die Untertasse, -n — saucer

der Urlaub — leave of absence

# V

der Vater, ⸚ — father

der Ventilator, -en — fan

die Verabredung, -en — date, appointment

verboten — forbidden, prohibited

verbunden — connected

der Vergaser, - — carburetor

vergehen, verging, ist vergangen — to pass (time)

verkaufen — to sell

der Verkehr — traffic; das Verkehrslicht, -er — traffic light

verschreiben, verschrieb, hat verschrieben — to prescribe

die Verspätung, -en — delay

verstecken — to hide

verstehen, verstand, hat verstanden — to understand

versuchen — to try

verzeihen, verzieh, verziehen — to pardon; verzeihen Sie! pardon me!

viel — much

viele — many

vier — four; vierter — fourth; vierundzwanzig — twenty-four; vierzehn — fourteen; vierzig — forty; das Viertel, - — quarter; es ist Viertel drei -- it is a quarter past two; est ist drei Viertel drei — it is a quarter to three

der Vogel, ⸚ — bird

voll — full

vom — from the, of the

von — of, from

vor — in front of, before

der Vorhang, ̈e — curtain
der Vormittag, -e — forenoon
die Vorspeise, -n — hors d'oeuvre
der Vortrag, ̈e — lecture

# W

wachsen, wuchs, ist gewachsen;
  wächst — to grow
der Wagen, — car
wählen — to choose, select
wahr — true
während — while, during
der Walzer, - — waltz
die Wand, ̈e — wall
wandern — to hike
die Wandtafel, -n — blackboard
wann — when
war — was (see sein)
das Warenhaus, ̈er — department
  store
warm — warm
warten (auf) — to wait (for); der
  Wartesaal, -säle — waiting room
warum — why
was — what
(sich) waschen, wusch, hat ge-
  waschen; wäscht — to wash; das
  Washbecken, - — washbasin, sink;
  der Waschlappen, - — washcloth;
  die Waschmaschine, n — wash-
  ing machine
das Wasser — water
die Weckuhr, -en; der Wecker, - —
  alarm clock
weg — away
wegen — because of
weg·fahren, fuhr weg, ist wegge-
  fahren; fährt weg — drive away
weg·gehen, ging weg, ist weggegan-
  gen — to go away
weg·stellen — to put away
weh tun — to hurt
weichgekocht — soft-boiled
weil — because
der Wein, -e — wine; die Weinkarte,
  -n — wine list
weiss — white
weiss — knows (see wissen)
weit — far; weiter — farther
weiter·fahren, fuhr weiter, ist
  weitergefahren; fährt weiter — to
  drive on
welcher — which
wem — to whom
wen — whom

wenig — little
wenn — when
wer — who
werden, wurde, ist geworden; wird
  — to become, get, grow
werfen, warf, hat geworfen; wirft —
  to throw
das Werkzeug, -e — tool
die Wespe, -n — wasp
wessen — whose
Westdeutschland — West Germany
die Weste, -n — vest
das Wetter — weather
wichtig — important
wie — how, like, as; so . . . wie — as
  . . . as
wieder — again
wiederholen — to repeat
Auf Wiedersehen! — Good bye!
Wien — Vienna; das Wiener Schnitzel — veal cutlet
die Wiese, -n — lawn, meadow
wieviel — how much? Wieviel Uhr
  ist es? — What time is it?
will — wants (see wollen)
der Wind, -e — wind; windig —
  windy
die Windschutzscheibe, -n — windshield
der Winter — winter
wir — we
wird — becomes (see werden)
wissen, wusste, hat gewusst; weiss —
  to know
wo — where
die Woche, -n — week
woher — where from?
wohin — where to?
wohl — well
wohnen — to live, reside; die Wohnung, -en — apartment; das Wohnzimmer, - — living room
die Wolke, -n — cloud
wollen; er will — want to, wish
das Wort, -e or ̈er — word
wunderschön — wonderful
wurde — became (see werden)
die Wurst, ̈e — sausage

# Z

zahlen — to pay
der Zahn, ̈e — tooth; die Zahnbürste, -n — toothbrush; die Zahnpaste — toothpaste

**der Zaun,** ⁀e — fence
**zehn** — ten; **der Zehnmarkschein, -e** — ten-mark bill; **das Zehnpfennigstück, e** — ten-pfennig piece
**zeigen** — to show
**die Zeit, -en** — time
**die Zeitschrift, -en** — magazine
**die Zeitung, -en** — newspaper
**die Ziehharmonika, -s** — accordion
**zieht an** — puts on (see **anziehen**); **zieht sich aus** — undresses (see **ausziehen**); **zieht sich um** — changes clothes (see **umziehen**)
**ziemlich** — rather, quite
**die Zigarette, -n** — cigarette
**die Zigarre, -n** — cigar
**das Zimmer, -** — room
**der Zirkus, -e** — circus
**die Zitrone, -n** — lemon
**zornig** — angry
**zu** — to, closed, too; **zu viel** — too much

**der Zucker** — sugar
**der Zug,** ⁀e — train; **der Zugführer,** — conductor
**zum** — to the
**zu·machen** — to close
**zünden** — to light; **zündet an** — lights, turns on
**die Zündkerze, -n** — spark plug
**die Zunge, -n** — tongue
**zur** — to the
**Zürich** — Zurich
**zurück·kommen, kam zurück, ist zurückgekommen** — to return
**zusammen** — together
**zwanzig** — twenty
**zwei** — two; **zweiter** — second; **zweiundfünfzig** — fifty-two; **zweiundzwanzig** — twenty-two
**die Zwiebel, -n** — onion
**zwischen** — between
**zwölf** — twelve
**der Zylinderblock** — engine block